GULBADAN

Babur watching his gardeners alter the course of a stream

GULBADAN

Portrait of a Rose Princess
at the Mughal Court

by Rumer Godden

Picture research by Helen Topsfield

M

Copyright © 1980 The Felix Gluck Press Ltd., Twickenham

ISBN 0333 30434 9

First published 1980 by

MACMILLAN LONDON LTD
4 Little Essex Street London WC2R 3LF
and Basingstoke
Associated Companies in Delhi, Dublin,
Hong Kong, Johannesburg, Lagos, Melbourne,
New York, Singapore and Tokyo

Designed and produced by The Felix Gluck Press Ltd.

Printed in Belgium by
Van Den Bossche Offset-Printing

Author's Acknowledgements

*I should like to thank, first of all, ShahRukh Husain
for her valuable advice on Islam and especially for her
description of the Haj; also Robert Skelton, Keeper of
the Indian Department of the Victoria & Albert
Museum, for the use of slides and workrooms. I am
most grateful to the India Office Library, the London
Library and the Literary and Philosophical Society,
Newcastle-on-Tyne, for the continued loan of books.*

*The poems (extracts) on pages 54 and 101-2 are from
Rumi, translated by Professor A.J. Arberry.*

استر با همراه برده مصحت و سلامت رخصت یافته و حضرت
پادشاه متوجه کابل شدند در آن مدت وقت تحکم کابل محمد مقیم
پسر ذوالنون ارغون که پدر کلان ناهید بیکم بود در دست
کابل را بعد از وفات الغ بیک میرزا از عبدالرزاق میرزا
گرفته و از میرزا عبدالرزاق مذکور عموزاده پادشاه بود
پادشاه بدولت بکابل آمدند دو سه روز قلعگی شد و
بعد از چند روز بعهد و قول کابل را بایشان دادند حضرت
پادشاه سپرده با مال و اسباب خود نقند هار بش پدر
خود رفت و فتح کابل در اواخر ماه ربیع الثانی سنه ۹
نهصد و ده بوده بعد از میر شدن کابل به نبش قند قند
و یکبار ه الجه کرده بکابل آمدند و حضرت خانم که والد حضرت
پادشاه باشند در نشست روزیتک کرده از عالم فانی بدار البقا
رحلت نمودند و در باغ نوروزی حضرت خانم را مانند صاحب
باغ که مردم و صیل اکه باشند کمر از نیکه منتقا لی داده گذا
درین اثنا فرمانهای سلطان حسین میرزا تا کید آمدند کما

The Great Mughals 1526—1707

Babur 1483—1530
reigned 1526—1530

Surviving sons

Surviving daughters

Humayun 1508—1556
reigned 1530—1556

Ma'suma
The Very Chaste Princess

Kamran

Askari

Hindal

Farukh
died aged 2

Alwar
died aged 4

Gulrukh
The Rose-Faced Princess

Gulrang
The Rose-Coloured Princess
Dildar's first child, born
between 1511 and 1515

Gulchihra
The Rosy-Cheeked Princess

Gulbadan
The Rosebody Princess
born c. 1523

Akbar 1542—1605
reigned 1556—1605

Jahangir (Salim) 1569—1627
reigned 1605—1627

Shah Jahan (Khurram) 1592—1666
reigned 1627—1658

Aurangzeb 1618—1707
reigned 1658—1707

The dynasty ended in 1857 with the banishment by the British of
the Emperor Bahadur Shah

I

Babur—Part One

She called herself 'this Insignificant Person' but she was not at all insignificant nor even just a person, though perhaps she was wise to call herself so because her name was Princess Rosebody, which sounds like someone in a fairy tale, but she was real, and of real and most dramatic times, being Gulbadan Begam, the youngest daughter of Babur, first Mughal Emperor of India. She was born in Kabul in 1522 or 1523—dates of births of oriental girl children, even royal ones, were not thought worth recording then.

If she had been born in London and not Kabul, Henry VIII would have been her King—he was given the title Defender of the Faith, just as her father, the Emperor Babur, would become Ghazi, Avenger of God. In England she would have had Cardinal Wolsey as head of her Church, but her religion had no Cardinals, not even priests—she was a Muslim.

Gul means 'rose' and there were many 'rose' princesses because the rose is the flower most loved and prized in the East from Persia to Hindustan and as far away as China. The Afghan rose is white while the Persian is the small pink rose called the Damascus or damask rose, sweetly scented, but it is plainly of the red rose that Babur was thinking when he named Gulbadan and her two sisters. The eldest was Gulrang (Rose-Coloured), the second Gulchihra (Rosy-Cheeked). Another of Babur's wives was Gulrukh (Rose-Faced)—and one of his slave girls, a Circassian, who was to be Gulbadan's friend all her life was 'Red Red Rose,' but Gulbadan—Rosebody – was 'rose' through and through as her name implies. Indeed, it might have been of her that the poet Hafiz was thinking when he wrote that 'rose is the colour of sincerity'.

A rose for Princess Rosebody

She lived almost through three reigns: her father Babur's, her brother Humayun's, and her nephew Akbar's, till two years before his death. Akbar was the most famous of the three, yet it is plain he was the one she loved least. All the same, if it had not been for Akbar she would have stayed hidden, a begam, or princess, amongst a thousand other begams and no one would have thought of trying to unravel the thread of her existence, a seemingly slender thread, tangled deeply with her family's; in the writings of her contemporaries her name seems always to follow in the shadow of another, which is perhaps what she would have wished, but some time in the years between 1587 and 1590, the Emperor Akbar 'issued an Order': 'Write down what you know of the doings of...'— he does not call his grandfather and father Babur and Humayun, but by the names given them by Muslim custom after death, different names, so that, mercifully, their mistakes and misdeeds would not be attributed to them when they had left the world. The purpose of the 'Order' was probably to help gather matter for the biography of Akbar himself, the Akbar-nama which his friend Abu'l Fazl was writing, and was given to three people: to Jauhar, who had been Humayun's ewer-bearer, which means valet, companion and intimate confidant and friend, to Bayazid, once Humayun's steward and a courtier of rank and, finally, to Gulbadan Begam, the only woman.

Probably not many ladies of that sixteenth-century Court could read or write, but Gulbadan, in her modest way, was a scholar: she collected books, had written poetry, but history was another matter.

By this time, too, she was in her mid-sixties and she wrote, 'When his Majesty (my father) left this perishable world I was only eight years old, and it may well be that I do not remember much,' but the Order was the Emperor's and, 'In obedience to the royal command I set down whatever there is that I have heard and remember.'

Obviously Akbar was disappointed; he was accustomed to the flowery ornate descriptions of such flatterers as the court poet Faizi and the poet's brother, the same Abu'l Fazl; they seem to have held the Emperor under something like a spell.

In writing his Akbar-nama Abu'l Fazl's preface begins:

'I, Abu'l Fazl, return thanksgiving to God by singing the praises of royalty and stringing its kingly pearls upon the thread of description,' and such description! That of Akbar alone, and only in the introduction, runs to five pages of phrases: 'unique of the eternal temple,' 'confidant of the dais of unity,' 'jewel of the imperial mine,' 'bezel of God's signet ring,' 'lamp of the tribe of Timur,' 'shining forehead of the morning of guidance,' and so on and on and on. Gulbadan's book, which she veiled under her brother's name as the Humayun-nama, opens with the, then, usual, 'In the name of Allah, the Merciful, the Compassionate'—from childhood, it is clear she was on confident, intimate terms with Him—then tells of Akbar's Order, her dutiful obedience to it, and goes on with grave simplicity: 'First, by way of invoking a blessing [on my work] a chapter must be written on my royal father's deeds.'

It was too plain and matter-of-fact for Akbar; Gulbadan seldom falls into the fashionable jargon or 'embroidery' and then only in a single phrase and almost always when writing of Humayun: 'his lily-dropping tongue,' 'that altar of truth;' for the most part her writing is so direct and unadorned that it is almost bald, nor did she have Babur's gift, shown in his Memoirs, for evoking in simple words landscapes, flowers, fruit and birds; her interest was in people. Her dates, too, are often confused and sometimes facts do not tally: for instance, she says Babur had eighteen children and lists only sixteen. For these reasons, or perhaps others, her book was only copied three times—there was no printing then—while Bayazid's had nine copyists and, of her three copies, only one seems to have survived, and that was lost for nearly three hundred years. Not one of the earlier historians mentions it, though Abu'l Fazl obviously 'lifted' parts for his Akbar-nama—without acknowledgement. Then, in the 1860s, a catalogue was made of more than a thousand rare books and manuscripts collected by a Colonel Hamilton in Delhi and Lucknow. Among them was this unknown little Humayun-nama which the British Museum bought from the Colonel's widow; but it was not until 1900 that Annette Beveridge, wife of Hugh Beveridge, the expert in Oriental literature, and herself a Persian scholar, had the idea of translating this Humayun-nama. It was a difficult and delicate task.

'There was just this one manuscript to work from,' she says in the preface. 'Some of the words were Turki which was the Princess's native language—Persian was an accomplishment.' The manuscript had, at some time, been rebound in plain red leather and one of the folios was in the wrong order: 'it has no frontispiece, margin or rubric...the end is lost...' but, as Annette Beveridge worked, beautifully enhancing Gulbadan's words by footnotes and a long preface, more and more did she come to recognise the value of what she was discovering. Akbar had been wrong. 'The book is unique,' wrote Mrs Beveridge, 'the work of a royal lady who lights up her women's world,' and, for all its simplicity, it has a certain majesty, the sure and gentle manners which could control tactfully behind the scenes even headstrong emperors; it is, too, written with a sincerity that shames other writers of the Court and, since its translation, more and more have historians come to rely on the Humayun-nama; more and more they quote Princess Rosebody because her memory was long and the scenes she recounts are so clear in their faraway truth that it is like looking down the wrong end of a telescope, not into the future but the past; scenes made small but vivid, and the first figure that emerges is of a small girl-child standing on the ramparts of the Citadel, her father's palace in Afghanistan's Kabul. She describes how the women used to look down from those high walls to watch their menfolk jousting or banqueting; but the gardens below were silent now, and she would have been straining her eyes to see a cloud of dust on the plain beyond the circle of hills, often snow-topped, that girdled the city; a tiny cloud of dust that meant a horseman or runner – a messenger from the father she had heard so much of, revered, adored, but hardly knew.

At two years old, perhaps three, she had seen Babur ride away with his horsemen, banners and pennants. He was always riding away. 'From the eleventh year of my age till now,' he wrote when he was thirty-four, 'I have never spent

Timur enthroned with Babur and Humayun

the fast or the festival of Ramzan in the same place.' Even after he had established his Court in Kabul, his womenfolk seldom knew, until weeks afterwards, where he had been, how he had been, how a battle had gone; nor did they know when he was coming back; once that was so unexpectedly that there was no time to put his little sons, Humayun and Kamran, on horseback to go out to greet him as protocol required for princes, even baby ones; it was not fitting that they should walk or toddle on ritual occasions, so they had to be carried pick-a-back by servants. Gulbadan, if she had been born then, being only a girl, would have had to wait in the haram until her father, the Padshah, came to her.

He had crossed the Indus into Hindustan before and won the battle of Bajaur, but this time, when Gulbadan watched him set out in 1525, he was not planning to return. He, who came from the far north beyond the Oxus river, now the boundary of Soviet Russia, was gathering his army to cross the mighty Indus again, this time for the real conquest of Hindustan, that fabulous and perilous land, as large as a continent, on which his ambition was set: 'For nineteen years I have dreamed of conquering Hindustan . . .' he wrote.

Babur was descended on his mother's side from Jenghiz Khan, on his father's from Timur-the-Lame, or Tamerlane, and in him was a strange mixture of the Mongol, the rough, adventurous, cruel nomads of the steppes of Central Asia, and of the Timurids, as cultured as they were brave. The word 'Mongol' had come to mean barbarian, and Babur would have been horrified to know that his dynasty was to be called Mughal; he was far prouder of his father's lineage and his bent, his longing, in all his hard, fugitive, wandering, fighting, early life, was for the culture, even luxury and civilisation of the Turkman courts, a longing he fulfilled—more than fulfilled—but at what cost!

'From His Majesty of the Fortunate Conjunction [one of Timur's titles] there was not one of the bygone princes,' wrote Gulbadan, 'who laboured as he, my royal father, did.'

This was true. Babur's two great fighter ancestors had

been great conquerors. Jenghiz Khan's territories went as far east as China and to the west through Russia, Poland, Hungary and Bohemia, while Tamerlane's empire at its greatest stretched from the Caspian Sea and the Volga to Benares, but each was so immense they could not rule it all and, after their deaths, the empires, divided amongst their heirs, fell to pieces. Babur's realm was not as far reaching but he became its Emperor; he truly ruled and on it he founded a dynasty that lasted almost three hundred years, yet even the great Khan and greater Tamerlane had not battled through such reverses, ignominious downfalls, poverty, illness, hardship, or risen from such obscurity, nor started as young.

Babur was born in 1483, the eldest son of Umar Shaikh Mirza, chieftain of the little state of Ferghana, a valley north of the river Oxus, now called the Amu. Babur wrote of his father that he, too, had been a warrior bent on conquest, but also that he was 'a plain honest Turk, not favoured by genius,' and happy to be settled in 'this fertile valley of grain and fruit where even the pheasants were so fat, a single one could make a meal for four men.' The Shaikh was fat himself: 'he used to wear his tunic extremely tight; so much so that, as he was wont to contract his belly when he tied the strings, when

he let himself out, the strings often burst,' but he was, too, 'of excellent temper, affable, eloquent and sweet'—a sweetness Babur inherited.

As Umar Shaikh grew more corpulent he retired to the old fort palace of Akshi and devoted himself to his pet pigeons. Pigeon flying was a favourite sport of princes and his pigeon house was built out over the steep cliff-like outer wall of the Fort. One day, as he was feeding and fondling his birds, the wall began to crumble—his weight had helped to bring it down—and Umar Shaikh was precipitated, with his pigeon house and his pigeons and 'took flight to the other world.' Babur, at eleven and a half, was King of Ferghana, the valley state he loved so well yet which was not big enough to content him.

There is one city whose very name through the centuries has seemed a call to the dreams of adventurous men, Samarkand—to men, not women who would first have counted the cost. Gulbadan says that Babur conquered Samarkand three times, 'twice by the sword, the third time without a blow.'

The first conquest lasted only three months. The boy king had already had to fight to keep his title in Ferghana, but still he set out for Samarkand and, after months of siege, took it. His soldiers naturally wanted loot but, 'How,' asked the young Babur, compassionate even then, 'is it possible to levy taxation on a place that has been entirely ruined and sacked?' Disappointed, his army began to desert. Some of the nobles offered to help him—on certain conditions. 'But,' asked Babur, soon to be nicknamed the Tiger, 'who could bear the tone of authority?' He would not listen, lost Samarkand and, coming home, found he had lost Ferghana too, usurped by his younger brother. He had to spend the winter in the little fortress of Khujand. 'He wept a good deal.' No wonder; he was only fifteen years old.

One alleviation was that, with the chivalry of the times, his womenfolk, taken prisoner, were sent to him, among them his mother who was with him through all his campaigns. 'I would not,' he said, 'on the strength of two or three defeats, sit down and look idly about me.'

Nothing seemed to daunt him, wounds, illness, not even the howling winter winds of the desolate steppes where he was driven to wander. For a time he was no more than a guerilla chieftain, often beaten, often on the run, lacking food, water, tents, horses, but after fierce skirmishes and battles he won Ferghana again, yet that was not enough; he had made a pact with himself to reconquer Samarkand which he did, but now he met the man who was to hound him for the next ten years; this was Shaibani Khan, one of the great tribe of Jenghiz Khan's descendants.

Shaibani Khan ruthlessly besieged Samarkand: 'It was the season of ripening grain but nobody had brought in any new corn,' Babur tells in his Memoirs. 'Things came to such a pass that the people were forced to feed on dog or donkey flesh. Horses were fed on mulberry leaves and shavings of wood soaked in water.' Again Babur's followers began to desert, letting themselves down from the walls at night and at last he had to arrange 'a kind of peace' with Shaibani Khan who laid down an added shame. 'Marry your sister Khanzada to me and there might be peace and an alliance between us.'

'At last it had to be done,' Gulbadan wrote as if she could not bear the shame either; the Princess loved this aunt, calling her 'Dearest Lady,' and hated to think of what had happened though it was twenty years before she herself was born, in fact early in 1501. 'He gave the Begam to the Khan'— in those days girls were 'given'—'and came out of Samarkand himself with two hundred followers on foot,'—no horses— 'wearing long frocks on their shoulders'—like peasants— 'and carrying only clubs'—no bows and arrows, spears or swords. 'In this plight, unarmed and relying on God, he went...'

Where? There is a gap in Babur's Memoirs, perhaps because this was the worst, the most ignominious time of his life: throneless—he had lost Ferghana again—he was penniless and disgraced.

18   *A storm in the wasteland*

در میان آنجنگه دوکنده باد امریک وشتی اتماده موسوم

به ما درویش شمسه درین دشت باوی ازو بر عنیان که شرق و رویه است

از انجا باد میرود و دوجنجد که غربی اوست و ایم زین وی می آید وشد باد وشد دارد

میکوسید که درویشی خنبی ژبن یا دیه یا وشد دوجار شده یکیک بر اناها قه بها در

ما درویش کفه کفه کفه تا می هلاک شدند

The party had only two tents; typically, Babur gave the one that was weatherproof to his mother. He also gave her his horse and would have had to ride a camel if his few loyal followers had not protested. He was wounded, may even have been taken prisoner, was for a time almost a nomad in the Hindu Kush, and his only sure base again had to be Khujand, which must have been a respite for the women. 'Its fruits are very good, particularly its pomegranates,' but Babur chafed there. 'It is difficult to support two hundred retainers in [this Fort]. How then could a man, ambitious of an empire,' he asked, 'set himself down contentedly in so insignificant a place?' He was Babur, the Tiger, a man of extraordinary charm as well as force, and his other followers came back— it seems in those days it was thought no disgrace to change sides, to desert a leader or prince; nobles and soldiers went where fortune seemed likely and, in 1504, Babur's turned— he had thought of Kabul.

The Afghan city's ruler, last of the true Timurid princes, and Babur's uncle, had died and the town had fallen into disorder with contestants for its throne warring against one another. This was Babur's opportunity but it was still a far vision; with his ragged followers and a small army of mercenaries, he marched for days and nights through the bare hills of the Hindu Kush, climbing the high ridges to mountains that, in the distance, looked deeply blue but, reached, were found to be bare arid rock, then descending into gorges, unbelievably steep, crossing glaciers perhaps, and wild rivers; one night, Babur, marching with his men, saw from the top of a hill what he had not noticed before, the star Suhail—Canopus—shining with extraordinary brightness.

'I said, "That cannot be Suhail." They answered, "It is indeed Suhail," and one soldier chanted:

> "O Suhail
> Thine eye is an omen of great fortune to him
> on which it falls."'

صبح نزدیک شده بود که از دامنهٔ کوه به منار سوار آییم

درمیان کابل و منار برف تازان اسب بود همه جا را

The star was right. True, Babur was never to see Ferghana again, the valley he loved so dearly where 'even the violets are elegant,' he wrote—elegant is a strange word to use for violets but perhaps these were the tall yellow violets found in the mountains of northern Asia and in Kashmir. Ferghana was lost forever but, when Gulbadan was born, Babur had been lord of Kabul for almost twenty years, was master in the north of Kunduz and Badakhshan and in Hindustan had, since 1519, held Bajaur and Swat; he had also held Kandahar for a year, and been welcomed back to Samarkand without 'a blow of a sword,' as she said.

* * *

Babur loved Kabul, then the centre of his domain. It stands, an oasis in a plain girdled with ridges of bare, red rock, hills almost fossilised that rise to mountains where the snow seldom melts, yet the city is fertile, a river runs through it and a line of trees marks the old canal. Babur had been pleased to discover a lake and meadows close below the Citadel which was of surprising height and enjoyed a beautiful prospect when the plains were green. In Kabul, 'there is a great abundance of fruit from citrus to peaches, damsons, almonds; its wines are strong and intoxicating but it is not fertile in grain.' Above all, Babur found gardens: one at the foot of the citadel, almost fallen into ruin, which he rescued and named the Garden of Fidelity; in another was a small natural hillock from which a stream of water, 'sufficient to drive a mill, incessantly flows. I made the stream straight and built a fountain but the turning of the millwheel is more soothing.' To Babur the Garden of Fidelity became 'the very eye of peace and beauty'. Later, in Kashmir, in the gardens of Nishat and Shalimar, the Mughals had slabs of stones set in a wide water channel carved so that the splashings and runnings of water made subtly different rhythms, but the water must run slowly or the subtlety is lost. 'Slow is of God,' runs the Muslim proverb, 'Hurry is of the devil.'

Kabul was rich in flowers too. Babur's favourites were narcissi and roses but here he remarked tulips growing wild

in the grass: 'I once directed them to be counted and was brought more than thirty different kinds.'

Kabul did not only give Babur beauty and security; it gave him a new self. All his rough wandering life—even his brief tastes of court fashion in Samarkand had been overlaid with war—his sensitivity must have told him he was ignorant; perhaps he even felt uncouth. He spoke only Turki; now he found, 'there are eleven or twelve different languages spoken in Kabul'—it lay in the great trade routes from China, India, to Turkey and beyond and was filled with men of every race, not warriors but merchants. It was Babur's first real knowledge of the world and its riches, but he was not easily seduced; he quietly assessed what, for instance, came up from India: 'slaves: fine white cloth'—the muslin for which India is famous—'sugar: spices: exotic fruits and birds,' but he found that the merchants were greedy, extortionate, and he was disdainful of them, as he was to be later, when he spent a winter in Herat with his cousins and watched the idleness and extravagance which came from their orgies of drinking—he drank himself but seldom so much as to incapacitate himself as a warrior and leader. Now he was more than a leader; the Tiger had learned how to rule and was on the way to being Emperor and, 'I ordered that people should style me Padshah, Ruler of Kings,' but a padshah had to have a court—and a haram.

Babur's first love, when he was only a youth himself, had been a boy, 'a lad belonging to the Camp bazaar, named Bauhari.' It was a passionate love.

> 'I was mad, deranged, nor did I know
> That such is his state who is enamoured
> of a fairy face...'

Babur never, as far as history knows, wrote verses for any of his wives. In spite of his predilection for Bauhari he had been married three times before the days of Kabul; at six he was betrothed to the five-year-old Princess Ayisha of Samarkand but, when they were old enough for marriage, they so

'...a fairy face'

disliked one another that Babur's mother had to 'drive him to her tent,' and Ayisha soon left him—unusual for a Muslim wife. His mother insisted he take another, Zainab Sultan Begam, but this was not happy either and she died of small-pox. The last was a young princess who had fallen in love with him at the Herat Court; that Babur loved her too is shown by his grief when, within a year, she died in childbirth and he gave her little daughter her name, Ma'suma,—Innocent. There had been another baby daughter, Ayisha's, who did not live—the countless baby and child deaths showed how hard life must have been for the women of those fighting chieftains.

To sire only two girl children, one of them puny, was humbling for a virile man but, says Gulbadan, 'in taking Kabul, he [my royal father] got a good omen.' An extremely good omen! An heir was born in 1507 and after this fifteen more children. Babur kept to the strict Muslim rule of only four wives at one time; the size of his haram was because, like other honourable princes, he took under his protection the women of any of his nobles who had been killed or taken prisoner in battle; this was to prevent the women being seized as loot; there were not only wives, but daughters, mothers, aunts, cousins, ladies-in-waiting, servants and dancing girls—some were even the women of his enemies. As the Quran—the holy book of Islamic rule—lays down:

> 'Men are the managers of the affairs of women . . .
> Righteous women are therefore obedient . . .
> and those you fear may be rebellious
> admonish them: banish them to their couches
> and beat them . . .'

Probably Babur never knew how many women he was responsible for but, as far as history can tell, he never beat any of them; the precept, though, that each wife 'must be equal in money, housing and intercourse,' he could not fulfil; Muhammad in his wisdom foresaw that and the same chapter in the Quran goes on:

Babur receiving tribute

'You will not be able to be equitable
between them be you ever so eager.
[but] God is all-forgiving, all-compassionate.'

The one Babur truly loved was Maham, his chief wife; he
called her 'My Moon,' and the first child to be born in Kabul
was her son. 'The name of Humayun—Fortune—was given
him,' and Babur tells that when his heir was four or five days
old, 'I went out to the Four Gardens to hold the feast of his
nativity. All the lords, great and small, brought their gifts.
Such a mass of silver coins was heaped up as had never
before been seen. It was a splendid feast . . .' and it was now
perhaps to forecast the future of this son that Babur took the
title Emperor.

The second wife, Gulrukh, 'Rose-Faced,' seems almost
to have been disregarded though she was the mother not
only of Babur's second son Prince Kamran, the trouble-
maker, and his loyal brother Askari, but of another healthy
boy and girl. Babur never mentions her, while his treatment
of Dildar, third wife and mother of Gulbadan can only be
called callous. The background of all these wives is unknown,
except for the fourth—and last—the charming Mubarika
Bibi who came to the Emperor in a romantic way. At a
feast given by one of his enemies during a campaign, Babur
disguised himself as a travelling acrobat and went into the
enemy camp, typical of his daring and sense of fun. The
daughter of the chieftain, seeing a stranger, courteously
sent him food and so captivated Babur by her beauty and
manners that he made peace and asked for her in marriage.
Bibi was popular in the haram, perhaps because she had no
children—always a source of jealousy, as Dildar knew to her
cost. Gulbadan, who obviously saw much of Bibi, calls her
Afghani Aghacha, the Afghan Lady, as against the Begam or
Princess for the other three, meaning that Bibi was not of
royal birth. The names Gulbadan gives her elders throw a
light on them: Khanzada Begam, Babur's sister who, after
ten years, had come back from Shaibani Khan to the haram,
was Dearest Lady or the Smiling One. Maham Begam was
My Lady, with an emphasis on the My, which was unfortunately true.

28   Maham was powerful, moody and spoilt and it seems

Babur denied her nothing. After Humayun's birth this queen lost all her babies which was not only heart-breaking but put her in a precarious position: to be the mother of the heir was a lasting honour but there was always the danger of illness, or even poisoning and assassination. Maham could not bear to think of Gulrukh's Kamran or Askari taking her own son's place, added to which, in the custom of those days, at twelve years old, Humayun had to leave the haram to be trained as a warrior and leader and Babur made him ruler and Prince of Badakhshan. Maham went north with the Emperor to install him but came back to an empty palace and her thoughts turned to Dildar, already mother of two healthy 'rose princesses,' and pregnant again.

Dildar Begam means Heart-Holding Princess, but she, it seems, did not hold Babur's, and when, on his way to the battle of Bajaur, the first fort he took in Hindustan, he had an urgent letter from Maham, he appears to have given no thought at all to Dildar's love and pride.

Probably as he read it he was thinking of other things: of strategy or of making wells and irrigation—always his passion—or, in his Babur way, examining flowers or watching the, to him, strange animals, a mongoose perhaps or monkeys at play. Maham's urgency was about Dildar's unborn child; 'Whether it be a boy or a girl is only chance, give this child to me,' it pleaded. 'I will declare it mine and bring it up as mine.'

Now and again a childless royal wife has adopted a child, usually from a good but middle-class woman, but never from within the haram, especially not from one of her husband's own wives, but Babur gave way, to Dildar's deep resentment. Maham also asked that her Padshah himself should try and foretell the sex of the child and, though he disliked and distrusted superstition, Babur again did as she asked. Two old women were sent for to the camp and used the traditional way of writing two names, a boy's and a girl's, on scraps of paper, rolling them in soft clay to make two balls which were dropped into warm water; the first to open would tell the sex. Babur sent a message to say the child would be a boy; it was. He was Dildar's first son but it was Maham who had the triumph of naming him Hindal—Hind because his father had conquered Hindustan.

29

It is understandable that Maham should have wanted Hindal but why little Rosebody? 'I was two years old when My Lady took me.' Perhaps Maham was still lonely, haunted by the children who had died; she knew too that, just as with Humayun, Hindal would soon be taken from her and the haram, and Gulbadan must have been an exceptionally captivating little person. Children of those high Asian countries are usually healthy and merry; the babies have skins like white-heart cherries, dark hair and black eyes, and beautiful little teeth, and Gulbadan might have inherited her father's good looks too: a face with fine features, straight eyebrows, straight fine nose, a sensitive mouth without the slight twist of Humayun's, and eloquent kind eyes. Looking at a group portrait of Babur and his heirs, it is interesting to see how the faces coarsened. Babur's is thin, fine-boned; Jahangir's, four generations later, is fleshy and sensual. Dildar probably had beauty, but it seems fitting that this most loved of Babur's 'rose' princesses should have looked, not like her mother, but him. No one knows; perhaps fittingly, as she wanted to be anonymous, there is no miniature or painting that gives even a glimpse of Gulbadan Begam.

Her book shows clearly how self-controlled she was— probably Maham's temper had something to do with that— but it was hard for a baby to be taken from her mother and family; she probably did not see her sisters again until she was old enough to go to the royal schoolrooms. It seems likely that the wives in Kabul lived in separate houses or pavilions with private courtyards inside the haram, a pattern that can still be seen in Fathpur Sikri; even aunts, cousins, concubines had each her own room, her little garden court.

There must have been good etiquette, even affection, between those Muslim women: there was, for instance, no 'naughty room,' as with the Hindus, in which a disagreeable wife could be shut up, or shut herself up. Babur, it is true, wrote of one such wife, not his own but one of his nobles', and added, 'May the Almighty remove such a visitation from

Monkeys at play

every good Muslim.' Obviously Maham never showed her temper to him and he had no idea how moody 'My Lady' could be.

Muslim babies then were not only loved but coddled; the tradition among the tribesmen and Afghans was that a baby did not leave the warmth of its mother's—or nurse's—body until forty days after its birth, so the bond was close and the child was lulled with security and love. Snatched from that love, little Rosebody must have known not only home-sickness but, worse for a child, uncertainty; probably slaps and kisses came equally her way, yet it seems only to have made her stoical; she was steadfastly loyal to 'My Lady,' but in those early days she must often have cried and though swiftly removed by one of her 'mamas'—a governess lady-in-waiting —she may have been heard by Dildar, who was powerless to intervene. There was no questioning a decision of the Padshah, but who knows what longing, as well as resentment, was hidden in this outwardly gentle lady; that Dildar was 'heart-holding' is shown by the affection and respect her children and half-children, even Humayun when he became Emperor, showed her, and her children seemed to have had the same lovable quality, especially Hindal and Gulbadan.

A haram in Mughal India was an ample spaced enclosure guarded inside by women warriors, expert in archery, reinforced by eunuchs and, outside the walls, by trusted armed men. At sunset all its gates were closed except one which had sentinels and was lit by torches; even women were searched when they came in, in case they were men in disguise. When the 'ladies' went in and out it was in guarded procession but, in Gulbadan's childhood, the haram at Kabul was comparatively free; the women were not veiled; they rode, went on picnics, followed shikar, practised archery and perhaps Gulbadan was allowed to join the boys in that play—in the East usually exclusively for boys—of flying kites.

The heights of the Citadel must have been a splendid place for kite flying. Oriental kites are made of thin paper, with struts of fine bamboo so that they are light enough to

respond to the least touch and are wonderfully manoeuvrable. Best of all are kite battles when the string is coated with a mixture of glue and powdered glass which hardens to razor sharpness. Folk stories of Jaipur and Jodhpur tell that this sport was popular long before the Mughals and in far off days, before there were law courts, disputes over land or money were settled in such a fight. Gulbadan, of course, knew nothing of this but perhaps her inherited fierceness, girl as she was, found an outlet in the feeling of a kite rising, playing the wind, and sending its throbbing message down into the bamboo roller on which the string is wound, turning it seemed almost by magic in the small hands that held it.

Kites were romantic too; often on feast days they would be tethered, left to stay steady some twenty feet in the air and a small paper lantern was tied to the string with a lighted candle inside, then the string was run out another twenty feet and another lantern tied, then another; sometimes there were as many as seven or eight lanterns, all softly glowing in fairy colours and moving gently as the kite stirred in the wind.

She would have had toys, the like of which can be seen in the miniature of her faraway ancestor Timur playing as a little boy at being a king; he had elephants on wheels, painted horses, small bows and arrows; the children in the miniature are all boys so there must have been balls, trumpets, drums —were girls allowed to share these too?

In the Court of Kabul, boys and girls seem to have been educated together, though the girls, sitting on cushions or at the master's feet, are always shown attended by their 'mamas.' The schoolrooms were furnished with small crossed bookstands for reading, tablets for writing—they must have used ink as Babur once sent Hindal a jewelled inkstand. The discipline was severe; in one school picture a boy is having his feet bastinadoed by another, while below a nurse is driving a small boy to his lessons with a stick.

The children would have learned calculating, poetry, reading and writing. Like men who have had scant education

The young Timur's 'courtiers'

Babur attached great importance to books; one of his greatest excitements was when he captured the Fort of Milwat and found in the library a number of valuable books. Characteristically, some of them he gave to Humayun and some sent to Kamran. Gulbadan might have known those sent to Kamran, as the Prince, though a boy, was still in charge of the women and, as can be seen later, had a soft spot for his little sister; perhaps, too, this was the beginning of her love of books. Babur wanted his sons to be versed in the art of writing; if he had not been so great and constant a warrior he himself could have been a true poet, as he shows in the parts of his Memoirs that he wrote himself—when he dictated he fell into verbosity and tedium. Even when Humayun was grown up, Babur wrote to him: 'You certainly do not excel in letter writing and you fail because you have too great a desire to show off. For the future write unaffectedly, clearly and in plain words which give less trouble to writer and reader.' How surprised he would have been to know that it was his smallest daughter who would be the one to follow him in this love.

Gulbadan certainly did not show off; in fact, she had few of Humayun's faults, particularly not his superstition; Babur, in spite of the star Suhail, despised astrology which had once cost him a battle, but it still governed much of the thought and action of the Court. Humayun was an addict, believing in dreams and omens; at ten years old he had decided, on going out for a walk in the morning, that he would ask the names of the first three people he met on the road and their meanings would show him his future life; everyone advised him to ask only one but he insisted on having his own way and seemed vindicated when the names of the three men he met were Desire, Well-Being and Triumph, but only the first could be said to be true: the second was severely tried and the last came almost too late.

Superstition contradicts faith and Gulbadan was deeply religious. The backbone or core of Muslim school teaching is the Quran and the children of that sixteenth-century royal

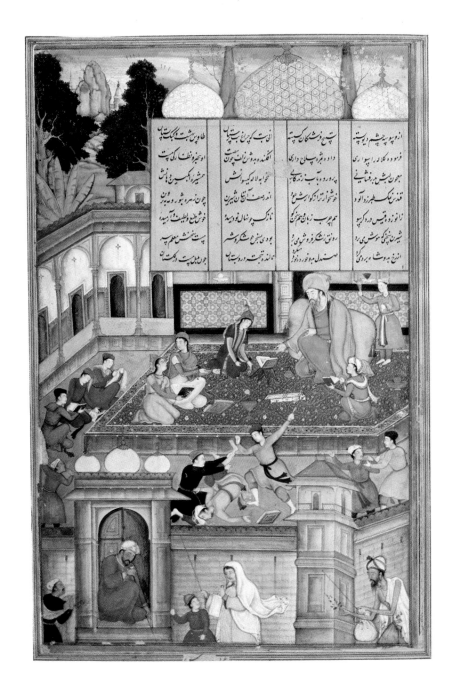

schoolroom were as obliged to learn it as boys and girls are now in all Muslim schools, even village ones where the children sit cross-legged on mats, rocking backwards and forwards as they chant, after their master, the sacred cadences; in some schools children have to learn the whole six thousand two hundred verses by heart, a parrot effect which usually blunts their minds for life but it seems with Gulbadan, every word of the Message sank deep.

Again, though he did not know it, she was following her father. Even on campaign Babur tried to keep the times of prayer. The Mughals were Sunnis—orthodox Muslims who pray five times a day, at sunset—the Muslim day begins at sunset—then night, dawn, noon and afternoon but on campaign there was sometimes no time to pause, which again Muhammad understood:

> 'Thy Lord knows that thou keepest sentinel
>   nearly two-thirds of the night,
>   or a half of it, or a third of it . . .
> Therefore recite of the Quran as much as
>   is feasible.
> He knows that some of you are sick, and
>   others journeying in the land, and others
>   fighting in the way of God,
> So recite of it so much as is feasible . . .
> And ask God's forgiveness;
> God is all-forgiving, all-compassionate.'

Absent or not, Babur was the ruling Presence in the haram at Kabul and the messages and letters brought by those runners from Hindustan were surely talked of over and over again, imprinting themselves even on a little child's mind. Babur's letters are vivid. There is one describing the night he was poisoned: 'Last Friday a strange thing happened. The mother of Ibrahim [the Lodi Emperor Babur had defeated], an ill-omened old lady, heard that as I had never tried Hindustani dishes, I had Ibrahim's cooks called in, and out of those fifty or sixty cooks four were chosen and taken into service. The Lady heard of this and sent for my . . . taster . . . Ahmad and, when he came, gave him a coin's weight of poison wrapped up in a piece of paper by the hand of a female slave. He took that poison to one of the Hindustani cooks in my kitchen, with the promise of...a gift if he could get it somehow into my food. The old lady sent a second woman to follow the first and see if she gave, or did not give, the poison to Ahmad...

'When we had finished the Friday afternoon prayers, the dishes were set out. I ate a good bit of a plate of hare, and fried carrots, and took some mouthfuls of the poisoned dish without noticing anything unpleasant until I took some of the pieces of fried meat. Then I felt sick... I retched two or three times, and all but vomited on the tablecloth. At last I felt it wouldn't do, and got up, retching all the way to the water cabinet. Never before had I vomited after food, or even after much drinking of wine.

'I became suspicious, and had all the cooks put under guard, and some of the vomit given to a dog, and the dog watched. By the first watch of the next day the dog was sickly and its belly swollen... One or two of my swordsmen had eaten of the poisoned dish, and all vomited—one in a very bad way. In the end all of us escaped.'

It was a treacherous act because, though it was true her son had been killed in the battle, Babur had treated the Lodi Queen with honour, even friendship, giving her land and a palace and putting her on the same level as his own begams. Even now he showed her clemency which seems unfair in view of the terrible retribution that fell on the others: the taster was cut in pieces, the cooks flayed alive; one woman servant was trampled by an elephant, the other shot with a matchlock, but the Queen was simply sent to Kabul. However, rather than face the haram she escaped from her guards and threw herself into the Indus. She was probably wise. The ladies of Kabul would have shown her no mercy.

That story Gulbadan must have heard again and again and read it in the Babur-nama but it is still remarkable that, as later historians have pointed out, her account of the important battle of Khanua is the best in any book. Khanua is not far from Agra and after Babur had taken that city the Rajputs rose against him. This was the battle when Babur defied the astrologer and made his famous speech to his army; the men were far from home, tired out with fighting, far outnumbered—against them were ranged perhaps eighty thousand horsemen under seven ruling rajas and some hun-   39 dred lesser chieftains with hundreds of armed elephants; above all the astrologer gave ill omen.

'At this time,' tells Gulbadan, 'Muhammad Sharif, the astrologer, said to the royal soldiers, "It would be best for the Emperor not to fight, for the constellation Sakkiz Yildoz (Eight Stars) is in opposition." Amazing perturbation fell upon the royal army. They became exceedingly anxious and troubled, and showed signs of cowardice. When his Majesty saw his army in this state, he ordered his men to gather together. One and all came—amirs and khans and sultans: plebeian and noble, low and high. Then he addressed them, and said: "Do you not know that there lies a journey of some months between us and the land of our birth and our familiar city? If our side is defeated—God preserve us from that day! God forbid it!—where are we? Where is our birthplace? Where our city? We have to do with strangers and foreigners. It is in every way best for each man to set resolutely before himself the two alternatives: if we win, we are avengers of the cause of God [because they were fighting infidels] if we lose, we die martyrs. In either fate lies our salvation; each is an upward stage in greatness."

'To this they all agreed. They swore by the divorce of their wives and on the Holy Book; they recited the Fatiha, the first chapter of the Quran and said, "O King! God willing, we will not spare ourselves in sacrifice and devotion, so long as there are breath and life in our bodies."

'Next morning which was March 16th, 1527, his Majesty arrayed battle on the hill of Sikri'—where, long afterwards, Fathpur Sikri was to be built. 'By the Divine Grace,' writes Gulbadan without embellishment, 'he was victorious...the flower of the Rajput clans were dead on the plain.' As a final disgrace a tower of the rajas' severed heads was built on the hill and Babur became Ghazi, Avenger in the name of God. At the time of the battle Gulbadan was four years old.

There were not only such victories; there was loot. In all his exploits, Babur kept so little for himself that he was called 'the beggar.' For instance, in the battle of Panipat,

before Khanua, the Raja of Gwalior was killed and his women brought their jewels to propitiate Humayun who was then with the advance guard; amongst them was the great diamond, now called the Kohinoor, rose-tinted; when it eventually came to Queen Victoria and was cut, it still weighed a hundred and eighty-six carats, 'and was valued,' wrote Babur, 'at half the daily expense of food for the whole world. Humayun offered it to me. I just gave it back to him.'

He sent too an enormous present of loot back to Kabul, telling the noblemen who brought it, 'I shall send with you some of the valuable presents and curiosities of Hind which fell into our hands. I shall write a list and you shall distribute them,' and the astonishing King found time to allot them with every member of the vast haram in mind.

'To each Begam is to be delivered as follows: one special dancing-girl of the dancing-girls of Sultan Ibrahim, with one gold plate full of jewels—ruby and pearl, cornelian and diamond, emerald and turquoise, topaz and cat's-eye—and two small mother-o'-pearl trays full of ashrafis'—an ashrafi was possibly worth sixteen rupees, a great deal of money in those days—'and all sorts of stuffs. To my elder relations the very plate of jewels and the self-same dancing-girl which I have given for them.' The elder relations were Babur's aunts, the first 'beneficent ladies' of the Court. 'Afterwards divide and present jewels and ashrafis...and stuffs to my sisters and children and the other harams'—those of the noble officers of his army—'and also to the nurses and foster-brethren and ladies, and to all who pray for me.' The gifts were made according to the list.

The haram could never have imagined such treasure. The Begams already had jewellery; almost all of them wore on their right thumb a ring with a tiny mirror, often set in pearls, in which they could admire themselves; they had necklaces, bracelets. Rubies were found in Badakhshan, turquoises and semi-precious stones would have been usual, but Turki jewellery of that time was of the rougher kind. The delicate Hindustan filigree of gold, the inlays, the brilliance

A princess showing her thumb-ring

of emeralds and diamonds and carved ivory must have added to the wonder but, in his usual way, Babur made it clear that these gifts were not simply for rejoicing; they were the harvest fruits of a victory sent from God, and the whole haram was to make a prayer of gratitude. It was to be a serious assembly. 'In the Garden of the Audience Hall a screen is to be set up for each Begam.' 'For each' meant that this was not to be a day's outing, but that the chief ladies would each bring her own establishment and camp in her own enclosure for what, nowadays, would be called 'a retreat.'

'When a pleasant meeting-place has been arranged, the Begams are to make the prostration of thanks for the complete victory which has been brought about...' Gulbadan describes it: 'Three happy days they [the Begams] remained together in the Audience Hall Garden...uplifted by pride and they too recited the Fatiha for the benediction and prosperity of his Majesty and joyfully made the prostration thanks.' Small as she was, Gulbadan made the prostration with the others.

* * *

Dancing girls may seem a strange gift for a man to give his wives but Babur knew, as all thoughtful husbands know, that if women live in a small enclosed world and are to be happy, there is a need for constant change, interest, recreation. This was the reason for the endless feasts for, as an instance, birthdays; when a royal boy was born, the ladies tied a knot in a yellow thread, and another knot was added on the same day every year; as the knots increased so did his weight and he was weighed—usually against money which was then given to the people with a feast. There was a feast for his circumcision too and, of course, for his marriage.

The women went on shikar, though it was only one or two who actually shot; they went hawking and practised archery, which must have been a beautiful sight, the ladies poised, upright, as archers have to stand, with all the strength of mountain women, their ample clothes blown in the Kabul

Court musicians

wind. One of the crafts of the haram was the making of archery thumb rings; some of the princesses made their own of silver, crystal, even horsehair, because in Persian fashion they drew the bow string with their thumbs. They watched polo from the Citadel walls, rode, went for picnics. There were games: cards, chess and a kind of ludo. Acrobats and jugglers could be watched, perhaps a snake charmer from Hind; there were jesters and storytellers and reciters, particularly one woman, Sarv Qad, 'Straight as a Cypress;' she was to make, as it were, a background of song and story almost all through Gulbadan's life. There was music for every occasion; the court musicians played flutes, lutes— long-necked or short-necked—cymbals, drums.

All this the ladies were accustomed to, but the Hindu dancing girls were more than a novel amusement. They were the first sight of a new world.

Highborn, or lowborn, Muslim women were covered from head to foot; they wore a long chemise with tight sleeves and over it another, but looser; indeed, sometimes, the royal ladies had four layers of clothes, open at the neck and hemline to show one below the other. The girls wore caps, often with tassels but for married women there was a high cone headdress, ending in a plume of feathers and from it hung a veil that was brought round the neck and fastened with, perhaps, a string of pearls. When they went out they covered themselves with long veils, fore-runners of the burqas or, as Gulbadan calls them, 'head-to-foot dresses,' though in the Kabul days the veils did not cover the face. Now the haram saw the Hindu girls in 'cholis'—tiny bodices fitting under the breasts, leaving a bare midriff—wide skirts but of gauze through which legs, though trousered, could be seen, feet bare as was the head, the hair sometimes in a plait left swinging, sometimes gathered in a knot circled with flowers.

The imperial ladies had thought they were versed in make-up; Timurid women used once to cover their faces with a white paste—it looked like a mask but kept out the sun and wind; this had gradually been reduced to a cheek paste; sometimes eyebrows were blackened and a red beauty spot painted on the forehead but now the ladies saw eyes, not discreet but eloquently used, made bolder with khol; palms of hands and soles of feet drew attention because they were reddened with vermilion. Everyone was accustomed to earrings but a nose-ring! The jewel in the nose-ring of a dancing girl was like a crest, an insignia, showing to whom she belonged, as each raja owner had his particular jewel; where these were precious, cut sapphires, emeralds, diamonds, rubies, they sent sparkles as the girl breathed and, as she danced and breathed harder, sparkled more seductively.

Undulating hips the Muslims were used to—belly dancing as it is called now was the mark of Muslim dancing girls—but they had never seen the subtle movement of neck and head and shoulders, the intoxicating movements of Hindu dance. Though used to music, the throbbing of the tabla drums was new and disturbing as were the tiny silver thumb and finger cymbals the girls used for percussion, and the tinkling of anklet bells, a music made with heel and toe.

The Prophet must have foreseen these seductions.

باز بها در بدست آورده بود و از ضامت و ناطق تمام حسر بها و بازار لولیان نظر اشرف گذرانیدند

و انحضرت بموجب مرحمت عالیه قبول فرمود و بعضی را باو عنایت فرمود و دو روز راو جهار روز درست کنو رو فرمود ه روز خود دیشنبه ششم خرداد ماه آلهی موافق شنبه دوم رمضن

The Quran advises:

> '. . .say to believing women that they cast down
> their eyes—not send those flickering glances,
>   reveal not their adornments . . .
> let them cast their veil over bosoms . . .nor let
>   them stamp
> their feet so that their hidden adornment
>   may be known . . .'

It is sure that Gulbadan, an intelligent six-year-old, would have watched and heard how the younger women of the haram were intrigued, the elders outraged, but she might also have seen another side. The girls would not have thought it mattered if she saw them weeping, she was only a child; or if she saw them shivering—Kabul would have been cold after India. She may have noticed that they could not eat the strange food and could not ask or plead—nobody spoke their language. They were as helpless as the parakeets Babur almost certainly sent in gilded cages, and many, like the bright-plumaged little birds, died.

In the long life ahead of her, Gulbadan was to know what exile meant and perhaps remembered those dancing girls, but now, even if pity stirred, there was, too, a great deal of excitement.

As early as 1527, two Timurid aunts of Babur had followed him to Hindustan, why, or how, no one knows, but they took their children with them and were met by Babur outside Agra where he housed them in a temporary palace. They stayed eleven months and it can be imagined what tales they brought back: of rivers so wide that the further bank could not be seen: of deserts and jungles: strange trees and fruits: bright birds not in cages but wild in the trees: of monkeys, elephants not for war but for riding: of insects, mosquitoes: snakes: heat: deluging rain, but above all they had been, and come back. Hindustan must have seemed suddenly close and perhaps it was no surprise when an order came from the Emperor: the haram was to leave Kabul and join him in Agra.

Maham, as chief wife and Babur's love, came in advance: 'My Lady, who was Maham Begam, came from Kabul to Hindustan. I, this insignificant one, came with her.'

II

Babur—Part Two

The journey was to take them five months.

* * *

Perhaps the visit of his Timurid aunts had made the Emperor realise it was possible for women to travel safely now through Hindustan. Besides, he was homesick: 'They brought me a single musk melon,' he wrote to Kabul. 'While cutting it up I felt myself affected by a strong feeling of loneliness and a sense of exile from my country,' that pleasant land of exquisite melons. 'I could not help shedding tears while I was eating it,' and he ordered: 'The ladies must set out within a week after this letter arrives, as a detachment of soldiers—guards—has already left Hindustan and will be waiting for them at [the frontier.] Delay will expose it to great difficulties.'

Babur, the nomad, could not see, once a decision was made, why it could not be carried out at once. A nomad, even a princely one, could always move swiftly: his riches were in tents—wonderfully lined, it was true but easily rolled up and carried as were his carpets; for furniture, there were only the heavy bolsters used for leaning against as the men sat on the floor, small tripod bookstands, probably folding, an incense burner against insects, a few necessary vessels. If he were royal he took with him the marks of his insignia: a scarlet canopy, banners and, always, the yak's tail—Babur called it a 'mountain cow's tail'—which, in every painting, is shown being held above the royal personage, male or female. Babur was uncommon in that he had a few books, but what was valued most were horses, good camels, guns and armour.

A camp could be ready to leave in an hour or two, but to pack up a whole haram, even in a week! Quite apart from 49 their numbers, the women could not move without chests of clothes—chests like the marriage chests still seen in India carried on poles. There were rolls and rolls of bedding, carpets, hangings, cushions, beds, low tables, stools, cosmetic boxes, mirrors: nets and nets of cooking pots, dishes, bowls, goblets, trays, musical instruments, games: all the paraphernalia of children from toys to schoolroom needs; pets and birds in cages must not be left behind, not to mention hundreds of servants with their own packages. Litters had to be made ready, both horse and camel and the lighter palanquins. It was soon apparent that the Emperor's command 'within a week' was not possible, which was, perhaps, why Maham Begam came in advance.

Babur's elder sons, the Mirzas—princes—Humayun and Kamran, were to stay behind to govern and keep safe the northern territories. Babur wrote to Humayun at Badakhshan cautioning him to beware of uprisings, to Kamran at Kabul to 'cultivate politeness and duties suited to his rank as a prince'—evidently even then Kamran was causing trouble. Mirza Askari was already in Bengal but Babur ordered that Mirza Hindal was to come with the haram to Agra. Much as Babur loved Humayun, for his fourth son he had an especial softness. He had recently sent Humayun and Kamran, on their marriages, 'ten thousand wedding presents.' Askari had had horses, weapons, gold, daggers, armour, but for Hindal Babur sent personal presents, that 'jewelled inkstand,' and 'a stool inlaid with mother-of-pearl, and an alphabet,'—he seemed encouraging the boy to be, like himself, a poet but, to woo him, also sent 'an enamelled dagger and belt and a short gown,' probably splendid, from his own—an Emperor's—wardrobe. There is no mention in his Memoirs or hers, of anything he sent to Gulbadan, but she did not expect anything, and to go to him, even as an appendage, really to see her Padshah at last, was gift enough for her. In fact, the journey must have seemed something of a holy pilgrimage yet, strangely, in her book she tells nothing of it until almost its end.

It seems Maham started in January, with snow and ice adding to the difficulties of the high Kabul gorge, the rough road leading through what must have seemed endless cliffs on which mud-walled villages stood, looking like forts—indeed they were strongly fortified. Every now and then, the river opened into small lakes that would have been, in summer, opaquely blue and all the time on the horizon were the mountains of the Hindu Kush, heavy with snow. If the caravan came by Jalalabad, it would have left the barren hills for an oasis of green, then on to the dangers of the Khyber Pass with its steep ravines and gorges where tribesmen could wait to ambush unprotected travellers, and here the ladies might have caught their first glimpse of the plains, misty blue from a distance but a doorway to a new land. Maham herself would have travelled in a horse-litter, something like a roomy hammock slung between two horses, or perhaps four, or sometimes, for a change, she lay in a palanquin which was faster because, when the ground was smooth, the men carrying the poles could travel at an even trot. In any case, the progress was slow; men often came down the Kabul river by raft, covering in a few hours what it took ten marches to do, but that was too dangerous for women. It is unlikely Maham could swim, as women could in the hardier days.

There may have been other litters or palanquins for the ladies-in-waiting and maid-servants, but many of them rode, it seems astride, and perhaps sometimes the little girl Gulbadan would have been allowed out of Maham's litter, to ride on the front of the saddle of a lady, a eunuch, even a soldier—soldiers were part of the escort; but it was the duty of the child Princess to try and amuse her 'Lady' with liveliness and chatter and try, too, small as she was, to distract her from the sadness of the death, at two years old, of the little Prince Farukh, born unexpectedly in 1525 after Babur left for India. Maham had longed to show the Emperor another son of their love but Babur never saw Farukh and Maham's disappointment and grief were piteous; probably, too, it exacerbated her temper so that Gulbadan's task was harder.

Travelling by palanquin

Perhaps the faithful Sarv Qad helped by singing:

> The breeze of the morn
> Scatters musk in its train,
> Fragrance borne
> From my fair love's lane.
>
> Ere the world wastes,
> Sleep no more: arise!
> The caravan hastes,
> The sweet scent dies.

Perhaps the soldiers sang too, marching songs, but the slow royal progress went on, day after day, with the cavalcade camping at night—it could have been sometimes in one of the serails Babur had built on the way—a walled enclosure with stalls for the beasts, a well and spaces for tents.

There would have been the sounds of a camp at night: horses stamping, cackling from the poultry carried as provender in nets, a watchdog barking and, further off, the eerie howling of jackals who would come in to scavenge after the camp had moved on. There would have been men's voices, subdued out of respect for the sleeping women, and the tread of the sentinels.

Smells, too, would have hung in the air, acrid from the cowdung added to the fires, and smells of cooking. Did Gulbadan steal out sometimes and look up at the huge Indian night of stars which made the braziers and fires of even so large a camp seem infinitesimal? She may have been too weary from the long hours of jolting and bumping.

As they reached the plains the weather would have been pleasant. February is still almost chill in northern India but the days are balmy. No one knows how the cavalcade crossed the Indus river—they may have been ferried over on rafts.

Babur had noticed how the land changed beyond this river; they were coming into the richer tracts of what is now Multan and the Punjab, to villages standing in fields of young wheat, small towns of almond and fruit blossom and gardens, towns in which they would have drawn crowds. Each day discovered more curious things; though Gulbadan does not mention them, there must have been so much that was new that any child's eyes would have opened in wonder. She was used to the beautiful meal-coloured oxen used in Afghanistan for ploughing, but here were water buffalo with horns three times as wide; there were monkeys, new birds, peacocks roosting in trees. She saw palms, cocoanut and date: sugar-cane, jack-fruit, papayas: betel and areca nut, banyans and banana trees. Had she ever tasted a banana?

At night there was the shrilling of cicadas, crickets and, almost certainly, the droning of mosquitoes. The women were fortunate if they had thought of nets; incense burners would have been put below the beds—a spring night in Indian homes, or camps, is always associated with that smell of burning incense.

It is possible to trace the journey by the letters Maham sent ahead, though even by swift runners they took a month or more to reach Babur. On April 1st he knew she had reached the Indus and been met by the military escort and his master of horse; the procession too must often have stopped for three or four days' rest with litter and palanquin bearers, horses and pack animals grown leg-weary. As they came nearer, so did the hot weather, bringing sudden dust storms that blinded, and filthied clothes and hair, but there was always dust and the strong smell of sweat from men and horses that not even Maham's perfumes could blot out. It must too have been stifling in the tightly curtained litter or palanquin.

At long last, on June 27th, they were only a few miles from Agra and Gulbadan at last takes up the story:

'When My Lady reached Kul-jalali [now Aligarh] his Majesty had sent two litters with three horsemen. She went on post-haste to Agra. His Majesty had intended to go as far as Kul-jalali to meet her but at evening prayer time some one came and said to him: "I have just passed her Highness on the road, four miles out." My royal father did not wait for a horse to be saddled but set out on foot and met her.

'She wished to alight, but he would not wait, and fell into her train and walked to his own house.'

'He would not wait.' Evidently Babur was deeply in love with 'My Moon,' so they did not want Gulbadan in those first few hours; also it was after midnight and so the little girl was left in camp. 'My Lady desired me to come on by daylight and pay my respects to him.'

Perhaps for the first time Gulbadan felt what it was like to be a royal personage. She had: '. . .nine troopers, with two sets of nine horses and the two extra litters which the Emperor had sent, and one litter which had been brought from Kabul, and about a hundred of My Lady's Mughal servants, mounted on fine horses, all elegance and beauty.'

'My royal father's Khalifa [vizier] came to meet me. My mamas'—her ladies-in-waiting—'had made me alight at the Little Garden, and having spread a small carpet, seated me on it. They instructed me to rise when Khalifa came in, and to embrace him. When he came, I rose and embraced him. . . . from Khalifa I accepted 6,000 shahrukhis'—the coin was worth about half a rupee—'and five horses, and [his wife] gave me 3,000 and three horses. Then she said, "A hasty meal—breakfast—is ready. If you will eat you will honour your servants." I consented.'

She had to consent—anything else would have been an insult.

'There was a raised platform in a pleasant spot, and a pavilion of red cloth with lining of Gujarati brocade, and six canopies of cloth and brocade, each of a differing colour, and a square enclosure of cloth with painted poles.'

'The meal'—more a banquet than a breakfast—'drew out to almost fifty roast sheep, and bread and sherbet and much fruit.'

The 'fifty sheep' were probably what they seemed to child-weariness, but there would certainly have been several whole lambs roasted in an underground oven and stuffed with flavoured chickens or goose or partridges which, in their turn, were stuffed with eggs coated with mince, fried and then halved; the whole lamb was served in a huge bowl of gravy made from onions, almonds, pistachio nuts and raisins. With it could have been a typical Mughal rice, long rice, flavoured with sheep's head, curds and saffron. The usual royal bread was made of finest flour, yeast, milk and sugar. The banquet was served on a low table, or a tablecloth spread on a carpet, and ended with trays of fresh fruit,

A morning feast

peeled, sliced and sugared, apricots, figs, oranges; perhaps, for the first time, Gulbadan tasted mangoes—it was the season. She probably enjoyed the fruit but sherbet is sickly sweet and the June weather, even in the shade, burningly hot. The small Princess had to sit politely upright, too—only boys and men could loll against bolsters; it was amazing that the little girl did not go to sleep, but her ladies-in-waiting stood behind her with a page perhaps holding the royal whisk to drive flies away, and if she nodded a 'mama' would quickly have prodded her charge upright.

'Having at length eaten my breakfast...'—sixty years later she still remembered that 'length'—'I got into my litter and went and paid my duty to my royal father.'

It was a moment of great awe; to her this stranger father was not only a hero, but Padshah, Ruler of Kings, 'the shadow of God,' as Islamic tradition called him. 'I fell at his feet...' but Babur was as kind and gentle with women and children as he was attractive. 'He asked me many questions,' she says and, gradually, she took courage.

For his part he must have been charmed by this unexpectedly clever and equally attractive little daughter so suddenly appearing. 'He took me for a time in his arms, and then this Insignificant Person felt such happiness that greater could not be imagined.'

* * *

Babur holding his Memoirs

Babur had found Agra 'repulsive.' It is difficult to imagine the city without the Red Fort or the Taj Mahal—buildings that have made it one of the most fabulous cities in the world as it overlooks the windings of the Jumna river. There was then no Pearl Mosque or Jessamine Tower yet it was Babur who laid the seed of these with his passion for beauty, gracious living and, always, water. 'Soon after coming to Agra,' he tells in his Memoirs, 'I crossed over the Jumna and studied the country to find a fit place for a garden. It was all so ugly and repelling that I left the river, disgusted. Owing to the forbidding aspect of the banks, I almost gave up my idea of making gardens there. But because no better place could be found near Agra, I was forced to make the best of this same spot.' He commanded buildings to be put up on the other side of the river, Gulbadan goes on, 'and a stone palace to be built for himself between the haram and the garden. He also had one built in the audience court, with a reservoir in the middle and four chambers in the four towers. On the river's bank he had a pavilion built.'

Babur had made gardens at Sikri as well, and at Dholpur, south of Agra; proudly he showed these to Maham. 'When we had been in Agra three months, the Emperor went to Dholpur. Her Highness Maham Begam and this Lowly Person also went. A [great] tank had been made there out of one piece of rock. He used to say, "When it is finished, I will fill it with wine." But as he had given up wine before the fight at Khanua, he filled it with lemonade.' A tank full of lemonade would have been irresistible to a small girl.

Those months before the rest of the haram came, when she and My Lady were so much with the Emperor were obviously exceptionally happy and, also, one of the few times Gulbadan writes directly of herself, instead of being tangled with the affairs of her elders. There was the time when her hand was badly hurt.

In the garden at Sikri, Babur had built another pavilion and, above it, a room which she calls a taurkhana, probably a mosquito-proof room, 'taur' meaning a net, 'khana' a room. One day the Emperor was in it, 'writing his book,' with, as it seems, his women in the garden below: Maham, with Rosebody, her ladies and, with them, the fourth wife Bibi. She may have come with Maham and Gulbadan from Kabul, though there is no mention of her, or perhaps she was with Babur already as she often travelled with him, even into battle, not because she was his favourite but, being childless, she had no ties and was probably hardier. She may also have been a little rough and it was she who hurt the child. 'I and Afghani Aghacha were sitting in the front of the lower storey [of the pavilion] when My Lady went to prayers. I said to Afghani Aghacha, "Pull my hand." She pulled, and my hand came out. My strength went and I cried.'

The consternation can be imagined, most of all in Bibi herself, because there was evidently deep affection between her and the little Princess. Maham must have interrupted her prayers, Babur his book. It is not clear whether the hand was dislocated or some of the small bones broken—perhaps the wrist had snapped—but Gulbadan does not make much of it. 'They brought the bone-setter and when he had bound up my hand, the Emperor went to Agra,' in other words, took them home. This is the first time Gulbadan calls Babur Emperor; it seems that it was now, in Hindustan, that the little girl began to understand what it meant to be a conqueror, a Ghazi, a Padshah—it was the beginning of her unswerving loyalty to the royal line and, all her life, more than anything else, she gloried in the privilege of her closeness to this, to her, sacred closeness. It was her right to call her Emperor 'Baba'—papa—and she knew his tenderness for her—but soon the halcyon days were over; word came that the haram itself was arriving.

At first all was peace; the procession was headed by Khanzada. 'My royal father went...to give honourable reception to my Dearest Lady who was my oldest paternal aunt and my royal father's eldest sister. All the Begams who had come with her paid their duty to the Emperor in her quarters. They were very happy and made the prostration of thanks, and then set off for Agra. The Emperor gave houses to all the Begams.' It is clear that the older 'beneficent ladies' lived apart from the main haram, as also did many of the cousins and kinswomen. 'In short,' writes Gulbadan, 'ninety-six persons in all received houses and lands and gifts to their heart's desire.' Not only that: 'To the architect his Majesty gave the following orders: "We command a good service from you; that is, whatever work, even on a great scale, our paternal aunts may order done in their palace, give it precedence and carry it out with might and main."' He used to go on Fridays to see them. 'One day it was extremely hot, and her Highness, My Lady said, "The wind is very hot indeed; how would it be if you did not go this one Friday? The Begams would not be vexed." His Majesty said, "Maham! it is astonishing that you should say such things! They who have been deprived of father and brothers! If I do not cheer them, how will it be done?"'

The haram, though, must have taken a great deal of settling, with many jealousies, arguments, even tears, and it is easy to understand the Emperor's feeling of escape when he made an excursion to 'the Gold-Scattering Garden,' with only Maham and perhaps Gulbadan's sisters and herself. 'There was a place in the garden for ablution before prayers. When he saw it [my royal father] said: "My heart is bowed down by ruling and reigning; I will retire to this garden. As for attendance, my ewer-bearer will amply suffice. I will make over the kingdom to Humayun." On this My Lady and his children broke down, and said with tears: "God keep you in His own peace upon the throne many, many years, and may all your children after you reach a good old age!"' but, as if Babur had had a prescience, or the accident to Gulbadan was an omen, the happiness was broken.

First, Prince Alwar, Gulbadan's small full brother and Dildar's only remaining son, her hope and joy, died.'Alwar Mirza fell ill. His illness led to an affection of the bowels, which grew worse and worse in spite of all that the doctors could do, and at last he passed from this transitory world to the eternal home.' The Prince was four years old, conceived just before Babur went away. Dildar could not stop grieving and, 'as her lamentation passed due bounds, his Majesty said to My Lady and the older Begams: "Come, let us make an excursion to Dholpur." He himself went comfortably and pleasantly by water, and the Begams also begged to go by boat.'

The boats were luxurious, with cushions, awnings, even

A procession of imperial boats

وریا منال آل ارباب اخلاص نظارت یافت و جراحت یافتگان روزکار را هم

شایسته پدید آمد

sails in the imperial scarlet. They were rowed by oarsmen in galley fashion or else driven by the heart-shaped paddles seen in Kashmir today, the boatmen sitting behind the curtained 'drawing-rooms' of the ladies. There was no tiller but a helmsman steered with a long oar and chanted the rhythm.

The gliding over the water, the air, the steady chanting seems to have calmed Dildar. Gulbadan does not say what Maham said or did. Was she contemptuous of such a frenzy of grief? After all, this was not long after she had lost her own Farukh. It was not that Babur was unsympathetic either—that he planned the excursion was proof of that—but 'due bounds' must be kept because these child deaths were only too common; hundreds of foreign children imported into India have died of dysentery down the ages, and not only children; soon Babur and Maham were almost put to this test of bitter grief.

When the haram left Kabul, Humayun, without asking leave, had followed from Badakhshan where he had been governor since he was twelve. He had stopped in Kabul to confer with Kamran and the two of them had sent ten-year-old Hindal to take Humayun's place in Badakhshan, an absolute defiance of Babur's order that the young Prince should come with the haram to Agra.

The Emperor was at first extremely angry. To keep his strongholds in the north and eventually push out beyond the Oxus had long been part of his strategy; now that was shattered. He could only send a chieftain to Badakhshan and give an order to recall Hindal.

Long ago Humayun's persistent disobedience had almost cost Babur the conquest of Hindustan; summoned to come with his army as quickly as possible to relieve his father, he had chosen to linger with his mother in Kabul and the battle had to be delayed, with nearly fatal consequences. Humayun was also now not a boy, but a man; he had been a father, though the child was short-lived. No wonder Babur was outraged but the anger did not last long. Humayun had only to appear for Babur to capitulate. 'I was just talking with his mother about him when in he came. His presence opened our hearts like rosebuds, and made our eyes shine like torches... The truth is that his conversation has an inexpressible charm...'

He had allowed the Prince to go to Delhi but soon the quiet days at Dholpur were interrupted. News came from Delhi that Humayun was seriously ill, 'and in an extraordinary state,' and the letter urged, 'Her Highness, the Begam, should come at once for the Mirza is much prostrated.' 'My Lady was very much upset at hearing this news,' and set out at once for Delhi, but Humayun was already being brought down by water. When they met, 'to her experienced eye he seemed ten times weaker and more alarmingly ill than she had heard he was...and the two, mother and son, like Jesus and Mary,' says Gulbadan, the only time she alludes to the Christian Holy Family, 'set out for Agra. When they arrived, this Insignificant One went with her own sisters to visit the royal angel of goodness.

'He was then growing weaker and weaker. Every time he came to his senses, he asked for us, and said: "Sisters, you are welcome! Come, and let us embrace one another."

'When his Majesty came and saw how it was, his light-revealing countenance at once became sad and pitiful, and he began more and more to show signs of dread. On this My Lady said: "Do not be troubled about my son. You are a king; what griefs have you? You have other sons. I sorrow because I have only this one."' Maham must have spoken so rudely out of distracted grief but Babur knew how to disarm her and, 'His Majesty rejoined: "Maham! although I have other sons, I love none as I love your Humayun. I crave that this cherished child may have his heart's desire and live long, and I desire the kingdom for him and not for the others, because he has not his equal in distinction."'

Though the doctors tried frantically, Humayun grew weaker and soon the women knew he could not be cured by medicine. They could only pray.

There has always been, in the East, a belief that, if anyone offers to God the thing most dear to them, and God accepts it, the life of a mortally ill man, woman or child will be given in exchange. The rite is simple: first a prayer is made, not only by the suppliant but by everyone who can be gathered to intercede; then the suppliant walks round and round the sickbed.

Babur offered himself. His vizier and his loved and trusted courtiers were horrified; Babur in exchange for a

65

Humayun! They begged their Emperor not to dream of such a thing. They would pray continually, they promised, continually reciting the powerful ninety-nine names of God and Babur should offer the great diamond, Kohinoor, most precious of all jewels in the world. 'What! Offer God a stone?' said Babur.

From that moment, Gulbadan tells, 'His Majesty walked round and round Humayun as he lay. He kept up that going round from the Wednesday and made intercession from the Tuesday, in anxiety and deep dejection. The weather had turned extremely hot and his heart and liver burned. While going round he prayed, saying in effect: "Oh God! If a life may be exchanged for a life, I, who am Babur, give my life and my being for Humayun."

'That very day he fell ill, and Humayun poured water on his head, and came out, recovered.'

* * *

Babur's fever grew worse; for two or three months he kept to his bed but, having given his promise, he made no attempt to get better. His followers could not believe it; over and over again they had seen their Tiger wounded, smitten with terrible illness, poisoned, always to get well again with remarkable speed. Now he turned his face to the wall.

As he grew weaker a message was sent to Humayun, who had gone back to Delhi, bounding with health. 'He came post-haste, and on paying his duty to the Emperor, noticed that he was very feeble. Filled with compassion, he began to break down and said to the doctors, "I left him well. What has happened all at once?" They said this and that in reply.

'The whole time my royal father kept repeating: "Where is Hindal? What is he doing?" He kept repeating, "Alas! a thousand times alas! that I do not see Hindal," and asking everyone who came in, "When will Hindal come?"'

Babur tended by his doctors

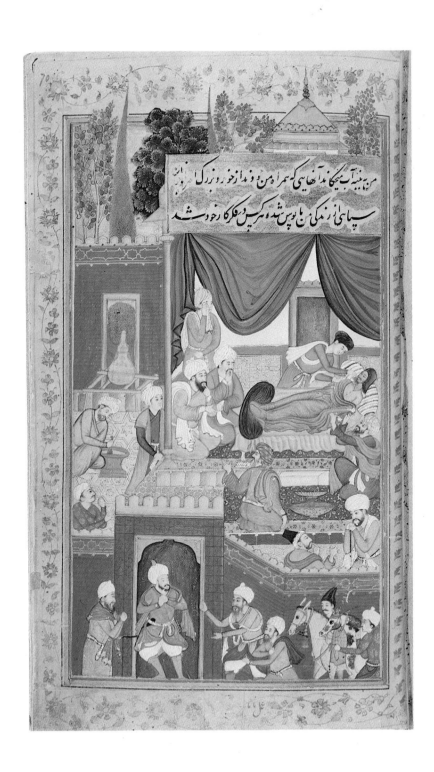

He does not seem even to have mentioned Kamran, so much more like himself than Humayun; nor did he ask for Askari though Askari was bravely fighting for him in Bengal. He had given them the full insignia of royal princes, the royal dress, a standard, a roll of kettle drums to be sounded when they went in or out of their palaces, the yak's tail held over their heads, but it is clear he did not really love them. Nor did he mention their sister Gulrukh's daughter or his first child, Ma'suma; he remembered Dildar's girls: '...he laid a command on My Lady, and said: "Marriages ought to be arranged for Gulrang Begam and Gulchihra Begam,"'—the Rose-Coloured and Rosy-Cheeked Princesses, Rosebody's elder sisters—but he never spoke of her. Perhaps he thought she was too young; he may have forgotten that, on his first faraway betrothal, the bride-to-be was only five, or he may have remembered it only too well and decided to keep his precious youngest from that searing experience. He named two Chaghatai princes but it was for Maham and, more importantly, Khanzada, to acquiesce or not—Dildar was not consulted. Gulbadan goes on: 'Dearest Lady, the Smiling One, said, "God grant blessing and peace. The idea is very good." The Princes, or Sultans, were sent for and conducted into the hall. Having raised an estrade and spread carpets and chosen a propitious hour, Maham...made both Sultans bow the knee in order to exalt them to the rank of sons-in-law...'

Gulbadan had need of 'the Smiling One,' because: '...his Majesty's disorder of the bowels increased. The Emperor Humayun broke down again when he saw his father's condition worsen'—already Gulbadan was calling him, Humayun, the Emperor. Day by day [his Majesty] lost strength and became more and more emaciated. Every day the disorder increased and his blessed countenance changed.'

'...He called his chiefs together and spoke after this wise: "For years it has been in my heart to make over my throne to Humayun Mirza and to retire to the Gold-Scattering Garden. By the Divine grace I have obtained all things but the fulfilment of this wish in health of body. Now, when illness has laid me low, I charge you all to acknowledge Humayun in my stead. Fail not in loyalty to him. Be of one heart and one mind with him. I hope to God that Humayun also will bear himself well towards men.

'"Moreover, Humayun, I commit to God's keeping you and your brothers and all my kinsfolk and your people and my people; and all of these I confide to you."

'At these words, hearers and onlookers wept and lamented. His own blessed eyes also filled with tears. Three days later he passed from this transitory world to his eternal home.'

Babur's death took place on December 26th, 1530. 'Black was the day,' Gulbadan wrote as if she shuddered all those years afterwards at remembering it. 'The Begams, the children and kinsfolk all bewailed and lamented; voices were uplifted in weeping; there was utter dejection. Each passed that ill-fated day in a hidden corner.'

For her it was a more personal grief than for most others; a small heart can love intensely and she had come to know her Baba in these months. Maham too must have jarred, she was so triumphant for Humayun. If Hindal had come in time, might Babur have wavered over the inheritance? As it was, on the next Friday, the Muslim Sabbath or holy day, 'December 29th, 1530, the Emperor [Humayun] mounted the throne and everyone said, "May all the world be blessed under his rule."'

On the same day Hindal arrived, too late.

* * *

Babur was first buried in the Garden of Rest he had made on the banks of the Jumna, opposite the place where the Taj Mahal is now and Maham insisted on every possible elaboration of the ritual: forty days of mourning, a day and night guard for the grave: sixty good reciters of the Quran engaged so that the five-times-a-day prayer could be offered at length every twenty-four hours, and 'My Lady made an allowance of food twice daily; in the morning an ox, two sheep, five goats: and at afternoon prayer-time, five more goats. She gave this from her own purse as long as she remained in the prison of this world.'

When she had quitted it, the Afghan, Mubarika Bibi, quietly took the body to Kabul and laid it where Babur had always wanted to be, in his Garden of Fidelity.

III

Under Humayun

'During the ten years after the death of his Majesty [my father] the people dwelt in repose and safety, obedience and loyalty.' This, unfortunately, was a rose-coloured picture which seems unlike the clear-sightedness of Princess Rose-body; from the opening of his reign Humayun was beset by what Babur would have called 'normal troubles,' but Humayun, ill-luck: wars and rebellion and treacheries that he could not or would not credit. His life, though, was brightened by the 'omens' in which he implicitly believed; in the end they did come true but they might have triumphed far earlier—in fact, his 'troubles' might never have arisen—had it not been for two great obstacles: the Emperor Humayun himself, his character, its weakness for opium, that and his brothers.

Babur had laid down that his affairs should be settled in accordance with Timurid custom by which, when the head of a clan died, his lands were parcelled out among his sons. Almost at once, Humayun was in difficulties with this Timurid decision, but he had given Babur his promise to 'Do nothing against your brothers, even if they deserve it,' which was strongly endorsed by the ladies of the haram. He would have been wise, though not as likeable, if he had done what the Shahs of Persia and his own Rajputs would certainly have done—put his brothers to death at the least sign of unfaithfulness, or even without that excuse; one raja, on his accession, just to make sure, ordered the murder of all his fourteen brothers, but Humayun, as soon as he was on the throne, gave the Punjab to his half-brother, Kamran, as well as making him Governor of Kabul and Kandahar; to the younger, Askari, the promise of Multan; to Hindal, his adopted brother, the country of Mewar which adjoined Marwar and Gujarat. He meant this to be a union with all four living in the peace Gulbadan describes, keeping, as one, the empire Babur had left; it seems certain he believed his brothers would.

There was in Humayun an innate gentleness, a trustfulness that was too naïve, even for a child—a burnt child at least learns quickly to dread fire—but not Humayun; for instance, it was a shock to him when he bitterly learned that the two men he had thought of as true friends, Sultan Bahadur Shah of Gujarat, and the Afghan Sher Shah were, on the contrary, his enemies—he had to fight them again and again. Humayun was brave enough, as he had shown in the battles he fought for Babur and again when, at last driven to fight Bahadur Shah, he took the Fort of Champaner, thought to be impregnable. After a four months' siege he ordered a night escalade of the Fort's rock face, which was so steep that some eighty iron spikes had to be driven in to allow the soldiers to mount. Humayun was among the first forty of the three hundred men who climbed—and this with the enemy firing from above—but, after such a victory, to the despair of his generals, instead of fighting on and consolidating his ground, he began the habit of spending weeks, even months, dallying in camp or in a conquered palace, hunting, feasting, listening to poetry, drinking wine and taking the opium he could not live without. It kept him benign and unperturbed; no wonder his ladies were lulled into security.

Perhaps, too, Gulbadan, when writing of those ten years, meant safety and peace in Agra, where battles were far away and the affairs of the Court and haram went on much as usual, though with increasing splendour.

True Maham had died. Jealous to the last, 'she said to me,' wrote Gulbadan, 'it will be very hard when I am gone that the Emperor Babur's daughters'—she meant her own adopted Gulbadan and Gulbadan's sisters—'should see their brother [my son, the Emperor] in Bibi's house,' or, probably worse to Maham, in Dildar's, but, of course, that quickly came to pass. 'In April, My Lady was attacked by a disorder of the bowels,' the old enemy, dysentery, and, like Babur, 'passed from this transitory life to the eternal home. The stamp of orphanhood was set anew on my royal father's

71

children, and especially on me, for whom she herself had cared. I felt lonely and helpless and in great affliction.' Gulbadan had grown used to Maham's ways and understood her and, too, was probably not sure how, after all these years of favouritism, her own mother and sisters would receive her. 'I was two years old when My Lady took me...and ten when she departed this life. Day and night I wept and mourned and grieved.' She was still uncommonly honoured by the Emperor's concern; he was mourning too—he had loved his mother dearly and so had a bond with Gulbadan and, 'His Majesty came several times to comfort me, and showed me sympathy and kindness,' she wrote. He may even have taken her under his protection because she stayed in Maham's palace for another year before going to Dildar's house where, it was soon apparent, she was loved and welcomed.

In that decade the Mughal Court must have been a wonderful place in which to grow up; it grew, too, in splendour and Humayun's imaginativeness and his 'inventions' were more and more amusing—and more and more expensive. Freed from the demands of Maham, Princess Rosebody, in her teens, had only her gentle mother and Khanzada, calm and reassuring, to rule over her. Her royal brother came and went; there was hunting and hawking, polo, elephant and camel fights, games and the continual feasts that gave him such delight.

One feast given by Humayun on the anniversary of his succession made such an impression on Gulbadan that she gives the whole guest list of begams and sultans. Two princesses especially impressed her—though almost grown up, she was obviously innocent—'They had great friendship for one another, wore men's clothes and had unusual accomplishments for women; not only archery and the making of thumb-rings and arrows, but these two played polo and went shooting.'

The feast was held in the house of feasting which had been set upon the river bank and was called the Mystic

Humayun resting while on a hawking expedition

House or Talismatic Place and which seems to have been built in octagonals. Gulbadan describes its splendour: 'This was the fashion of the Mystic House: in the large octagonal hall was set the jewelled throne which My Lady [now Khanzada] had given for the feast and which was placed in the forecourt of the house, and a gold-embroidered divan was laid in front of it [on which] his Majesty and Dearest Lady sat together...and above and below it were spread out hangings embroidered with gold, and wonderful strings of pearls hung, each 1½ yards in length...

'In the small octagonal room, in an alcove, were set a gilded bedstead and pān-dishes'—the Court had evidently taken to the Hindu habit of chewing pān leaves folded with a paste of areca nut. 'There were water-vessels and jewelled drinking-vessels, and utensils of pure gold and silver.

'Facing west [was] the audience hall; facing east, the garden... There were three houses...one they named the House of Dominion, and in it were military appurtenances, such as jewelled scimitars and gilded armour, a broad dagger and a curved dagger, and a quiver, all gilt, and a gold-embroidered overmantle...

'In the second, called the House of Good Fortune, an oratory had been arranged, and books placed, and gilded pencases, and splendid portfolios, and entertaining picture-books written in beautiful characters.' Humayun, with his love of poetry, attached enormous importance to his library. One of his later 'miracles' or omens was when, after he had lost almost all his possessions and his army was scattered and he was wandering in the desert, a solitary pack-camel appeared; it was laden with his most precious books.

'In the third room of the Mystic House, which they called the House of Pleasure, were set out a gilded bedstead and a coffer of sandalwood, and all imaginable pillows. Then in front were spread tablecloths, all of gold brocade. Various fruits and beverages had been got ready. Then the viands of the feast were set forth,' writes Gulbadan.

There would have been the same stuffed and roasted sheep as at Gulbadan's childhood feast, chicken spit-roasted with herbs or cooked in a tandur—an earthenware oven buried in the earth: meat balls, sometimes stuffed with apricots, a choice of breads: rice cooked in ghi—a sort of butter—and flavoured with fragrant black cummin-seed known as 'imperial cummin-seed,' or the rice would be coloured yellow with saffron soaked in milk. Sweet-meats were covered in silver, ground to a powder and formed into sheets so soft and fine they had to be held between paper until they were spread. There would have been vegetables, nuts, lentils, raisins, cooked in every imaginable way; sometimes there was an all white menu. 'Robes of honour were put on, gifts bestowed, and head-to-foot dresses given...' The head-to-foot dresses served the purposes of masks or fancy dress and so the young people could behave as they chose. They also ate comfits. The comfit probably had ma'jun, which is an intoxicant, in it, so that they became even more excited, and even Khanzada, the dignified Dearest Lady, thought it fun. Players made music. Also, a woman's bazaar had been arranged, and boats had been decorated. 'One boat was made in the semblance of an upper room, and below it was a garden that was a little paradise of flowers.'

'In short, everyone was astonished and amazed who beheld what gift of contrivance the great God had bestowed on the blessed mind of his Majesty.'

Then there was the feast for Hindal's first wedding, given by Khanzada when the Prince married her adopted daughter—Khanzada had now no children of her own. She made a most entertaining and amusing feast and the bride was given presents 'such as had not been seen,' writes Gulbadan, 'for any child of my royal father.' She enumerates almost everything from 'nine jackets with garniture of jewelled balls [or buttons], one of ruby, one of cornelian, one of emerald, one of turquoise, one of cat's eye. Necklaces, nine, earrings of rubies, others of pearl: three fans, one royal umbrella,' right down to gold and silver vessels, horses, slaves, and ending with 'three head of elephant.'

It was in these early years, too, that Humayun went as far as laying the foundation stone of a new capital, another city of Delhi, and building had begun. How could a member of such a haram feel anything but enjoyment and security, especially a girl just blooming into what was obviously great attractiveness?

Tuesdays and Thursdays were Court days, and when the Emperor was in Agra camps were set up in the countryside roundabout for hunts and feastings, and the tents of Babur's widows and children were pitched in 'places of honour,' higher than Humayun's own haram, but soon, inevitably, the camps were not for pleasure but for battle. There were no more 'Court Days!'

In the February of 1534 the Emperor unwillingly set out from that favourite place of peace, the Gold-Scattering Garden, and marched with his army against Bahadur Shah who, after defeat, fled to Champaner, the fortress where Humayun made his extraordinarily courageous night assault and triumphantly took the Fort; then he heard that, in his absence, Prince Askari was conspiring to usurp him at Agra. Humayun seized the excuse to come back to his capital where he stayed a year, a fatal year which gave his other foe, the Afghan Sher Shah, time to gather his forces.

Unaware of this danger, Humayun set out again, meaning to extend his realm as an ambitious emperor should and, in 1537, took Benares and went on to Gaur—Bengal—where he was again successful, but where, once again, he dallied; so much so that, after the first month there, the Emperor's generals never saw him, as he stayed shut in his palace, devoting himself to poetry, music, dancing girls and his favourite drug. 'I am an opium-eater,' he once said disarmingly. 'If there is delay in my coming and going, do not be angry with me.' There was far too much delay and Gulbadan's next sad description is of another brother's rebellion, grievously that of her own full brother Hindal.

Hindal, now eighteen, had been left to keep communications open with Agra but deserted his post, installed himself at Agra and killed the venerable and trusted messenger Humayun sent to him. Worst of all to Gulbadan and the elder ladies, Hindal read the Khutba, the sacred sermon of the Muslim Sabbath, Friday, in the royal palace, a privilege that belonged only to the sovereign, which meant that Hindal was proclaiming himself Emperor.

This did rouse Humayun; at once he left Gaur for Agra but he was cumbered by his haram. Long ago, in Hindustan,

Celebration of a marriage

Babur had learned the wisdom of no longer taking his women folk into battle. Gone were the days when the Timurid ladies could ride for long hours, endure a chase, the hardihood of being taken prisoner and the simplicity in those days of camp life. Though Humayun took only his own personal haram, his pampered darlings needed an elaborate train of luxury and followers, a procession slow to move and always conspicuous. He made, too, the error of bringing them up from Gaur by boat which added to the dangers because, camping on the bank at night, when attacked on the shore they were cut off from retreat by the river Ganges, and it was now that Sher Shah pounced.

'Such was God's will,' wrote Gulbadan, 'they halted without precaution. Sher Shah came and fell upon them and the army was defeated. His Majesty's blessed head was wounded.' They struggled on to Chausa—a river port—'and Sher Shah came again and inflicted another blow.' It was a blow of shame. Sher Shah, to do him justice, tried to defend the haram but could not restrain his followers and, for the first time in a Mughal battle, women and children were killed or lost. 'Of many who were in that rout,' Gulbadan tells in shame and sorrow, 'there was never heard, in any way soever, news or sign.' Among them were two of Humayun's wives and his only remaining child, the little Princess Aqiqa, six years old. 'He never heard a word as to whether they were drowned or what became of them.'

Wounded, bereft and sick at heart, Humayun managed to get back to Agra. When Hindal heard that the real Emperor was coming, he fled to Delhi where he was seized by Kamran who had come down from Kabul on the pretence of conferring with Humayun but in reality to see if the time was ripe to proclaim himself King of Kabul and the North.

Kamran stayed in the Rose-Scattering Garden; 'scattering' seems a favourite word for Mughal gardens, but history does not say if gold or even roses were ever scattered in them; there was a custom, though, when, later, the Mughals conquered Kashmir, that on their visits, thousands of roses were floated down the Jhelum to greet the emperors as they approached Srinagar.

Kamran 'waited' upon the stricken Emperor as did the senior or beneficent court ladies whose dismay must have been intense—they were used to battles won, not lost. With them was Gulbadan, now seventeen years old. 'He [the Emperor] took notice of this Insignificant One, and was kindly pleased to say: "I did not know you at first, because when I led the army to Gaur, you wore the cap, and now, when I saw the high muslin coif I did not recognise you."'

This is the first indication the Princess gives that she was married: married women always wore the high coif with its veil and ornaments of pearl and feathers. Gulbadan's husband was Khizr Khwaja Khan, a grandee of Humayun's Court. She herself tells nothing about him; to her, even her husband was obviously of little importance compared to the royal line and she only once gave the name of a son, Saadat Yar, and that was when Hindal was killed and she wrote that she wished Saadat Yar had died instead of the Mirza; now her thoughts were all with Humayun who, when he saw her, did more than take notice of her; he poured out his grief.

'He said: "Oh, my Gulbadan, I used very often to think of you, and was sometimes sorry, and said: 'I do wish I had brought her.' But at the time of the disaster I was thankful I had not, and I said: 'Thank God I did not bring Gulbadan.' For although Aqiqa was young, I have been consumed by a hundred thousand regrets and cares, and have said: 'Why did I take her with the army?'" but he was still the forgiving brother, ready to forgive treachery, even usurpation.

'A few days later he came to see my mother. He had with him the Holy Book [the Quran]. He commanded the attendants to retire for a while, and they rose and there was privacy. Then he said to Dildar Begam and this Insignificant One: "May what I do be right... There is no anger in my heart against Hindal. If you do not believe it..." he had lifted up the Holy Book when her Highness my mother and this Poor Thing snatched it from his hand.

'Then again he spoke: "How would it be, Gulbadan, if you went yourself and fetched your brother Hindal?" Her Highness, my mother, said: "This girl is young. She has never made a journey [alone]. If you approve, I would go." His Majesty said: "...If you would honour him with a visit, it would be a healing-balm applied for us all."

'Then he sent her Highness, my mother, to fetch Mirza Hindal.'

News came that Sher Shah was advancing towards Lucknow. There was no time to lose, yet once again Humayun delayed for what must have seemed to his army, his generals, his advisers and relations a ludicrous whim. At the debacle at Chausa when Humayun tried to cross the river, his horse had sunk under him and he would have drowned had he not been rescued by a humble water-carrier who floated the Emperor to safety on the inflated buffalo skin used to carry water. Humayun, in his emotion, was so grateful that he promised the water-carrier that he should sit on his, the Emperor's, throne and, at this inopportune moment, the man appeared to claim his promise; in spite of all protests, Humayun kept his word. Even Gulbadan did not approve. 'To cut the story short,' she says curtly, 'His Majesty made the water-carrier servant sit on the throne, and ordered all the amirs to make obeisance to him. The servant gave everyone what he wished, and made appointments. For as much as two days the Emperor gave royal power to that menial. Mirza Hindal was not present...he had gone to Alwar with the intention of getting arms ready. Neither did Mirza Kamran appear...outraged, he sent to say to his Majesty: "Gifts and favours of some other kind ought to be the servant's reward. What propriety is there in setting him on the throne? At a time when Shir Khan [Sher Shah] is near, what kind of affair is this to engage your Majesty?"' But Humayun would not listen and went on with what they could only call 'his antics,' while Sher Shah steadily advanced.

At last the Emperor set out to meet this formidable enemy, leaving Kamran to act for him at Agra, but Kamran thought it better, certainly for himself, to retreat to Lahore. He took Gulbadan with him—he had been ill and said he needed her, but it may also have been that he wanted the services of her husband. Gulbadan protested violently but, 'he took me by main force, with a hundred weepings and complaints and laments, [took me] away from my mother and my sisters, and my father's people, and my brothers, and parted us who had all grown up together from infancy.

Nizam the water-carrier helping Humayun to cross the Ganges

واتفرست ـ بامیرزاعپکری معدودی جندالغارکرده بداراخلافت اکره

نزول اجلال خمود زده ومیرزا عالی یوسی آبستان کامران آبستان روسی عالی سرفراز شد وبعد از چند روز میرزا سندال وسپه بیته بهم هرا
وبالغیبن واجل اونسرند وسپر افکند از الوراهد ملازرت نمود وانخصرت بمتضای مراحم ذاتی نوارش وم منوقفته
ویلم اوسی لوبناورد ورد وتعقیدات بی پایان که از انداز وشبری پاده باش دش امدر جون نیکهان ازروی بی تهیری
امری سرنوشت بطور آمد هموار در نتارک این امری یوخود در انجام آورت ـ وادوات تلافی اشعناء اش شند
الزراط اعم ملکت ادراوسپاسپیان استیام عتبه علیه مشرف می شندند دین اشاپشقای پاک سرشت بامیداوه

'I saw that the Emperor's command also was in the affair. I was helpless. I wrote a suppliant letter, saying: "I never expected your Majesty to cut off this Insignificant One from your service, and to give her to Mirza Kamran." To this humble note he sent a compassionate answer to this effect: "I had no heart to part with you, but the Mirza persisted, and was miserable, and begged very hard, and I was obliged to trust you to him for just now there is important work on hand. God willing, I will send for you when it is settled."

'When the Mirza was starting, many people, amirs and traders and so on, made preparation with the intention of letting their wives and families march under his escort to Lahore. When we reached [the city] news came of a battle on the Ganges, and that a defeat had befallen the royal army.' This was the battle of Khanarij and a heavy defeat indeed.

The rest of the haram, under the escort of Hindal who showed much bravery, made a difficult way to Lahore where the Emperor arrived as well, but every day came news of Sher Shah's advance; he took Agra where he set up a new dynasty and then came in hot pursuit. Humayun sent him a message: 'I have left you the whole of Hindustan. Leave Lahore alone,' but that unjust man, as Gulbadan calls him, 'fearless of God, answered, "I have left you Kabul. Go there."'

'As soon as the Shah's message came,' wrote Gulbadan, 'it was like the Day of Resurrection. People left their decorated places [palaces?] and furniture just as they were, but took with them whatever money they had. There was thankfulness to God, because mercifully a ford was found across the Lahore water where everyone crossed.'

It was a mass exodus; the leaders of the royal army were filled with gloom and apprehension; their men were beaten and weary, and they had the long train of helpless women and children and a ragged band of camp followers; it was now that Humayun's advisers urged him to seize Kamran and put him to death while there was still time and the Prince was near enough, but again Humayun refused. In any case it is doubtful if he could have succeeded; Kamran had twelve thousand men and Askari was soon to desert the Emperor again in favour of his blood brother and take his army with him. Even Hindal, after Humayun's generous forgiveness, deserted too and went to Multan.

In fact, Humayun soon found he could not do as Sher Shah had suggested and go to Kabul; the royal progress through the Punjab ended where the road forks, north west for Kabul, south west for Sind. Kamran, with his greater and fresher force blocked the Kabul road and Humayun was forced to go south. The cavalcade split and nobles and soldiers had to choose whom to follow.

The women had no choice; they were 'apportioned,' but for those whose litters turned south towards Sind, taking them on a strange and frightening road, far from their known and loved home, it must have been bitter. Dildar had gone with Hindal to Multan, Khanzada stayed with Humayun though later she was sent as an ambassador from Sind to Kandahar, but Gulbadan was again taken by Kamran, this time to Kabul.

He treated her kindly, not at all as he behaved to the other royal ladies whom he would not allow to come back to their houses in the city, and deprived of their purses and allowances; Gulbadan had her own palace; it seems too that her husband was with her and it is likely that it was during this forced stay with Kamran that her children were born. Though, in her chosen fashion, she does not mention their advent, she had at least two sons and a daughter, if not more. Her days must have been full; she had many family friends in Kabul and, later on, Hindal arrived, though as a shamed prisoner on parole. With him came Dildar, so that the family were reunited, but it can be guessed that Gulbadan shrank from Kamran and not only because he was high handed and atrociously cruel; for Gulbadan the Emperor was divine; she could not understand the Princes' treachery. Evidently, too, her husband had fulfilled Kamran's hope and was on his side—to her an even deeper betrayal.

What Gulbadan said to the Khan is not known but it must have been continual reproach, especially in those terrible years when month after month Kamran's runners came in telling of the ignominy and stark poverty her Emperor was enduring in Sind; the more Kamran gloried in the news, the more she must have grieved.

Humayun, though, never lost his strange optimism; he had a pet white cockerel whose duty it was to wake him with its crowing for the time of dawn-prayer and if it perched on his shoulder he knew the day was lucky, no matter if it seemed to be the contrary.

For Gulbadan too, out of this desolate time, two people were to come who were to be as important in her life as her father and Khanzada; one was Hamida Banu Begam, Humayun's new wife; the other, Hamida's son, Akbar.

'My Lady, who was Maham Begam,' Gulbadan wrote of this, 'had [always had] a great longing and desire to see a son of Humayun.' In his early days he had had a son born in Badakhshan but the child died before Maham had a chance to see him; in fact, she never saw a son of Humayun's; it was long after her death that Humayun met Hamida.

It happened when he was first in Sind and made a detour to see Hindal in Multan—perhaps hoping to win the Prince and his army back to help him. Dildar was with Hindal; Gulbadan writes of this as if she were present, but she was far away in Kabul; probably Dildar told her about it and Hamida too, when they became familiars.

Dildar had given a feast for the Emperor which seems strange in that time of stress and deprivation, but it must be remembered that, in the beginning, two hundred thousand people went with Humayun into Sind, so that, at that time, there was still a Court with some of a Court's resources and Dildar, the Heart-Holding Princess, knew how to please an emperor, though she little dreamed how romantically she would please this one: 'As soon as he saw Hamida Banu Begam,' as Gulbadan calls her, 'he asked who she was.'

Humayun, it seems, had never been particularly interested in his wives and concubines, letting Maham choose for him. Now he chose for himself. It was an extraordinary and unpropitious moment for him to fall in love; he was war-worn, disillusioned, an emperor without an empire, a king without a throne, and so poor that he could not even pay the dowry, or settlement, with which, under Muslim law, a husband must endow each wife. There was, too, opposition; the first objections came from Hindal who plainly wanted to marry Hamida himself. It was he who brought up the question

A cockerel perching on Humayun's shoulder

of the dowry: 'Your Majesty is a king. Heaven forbid there should not be a proper settlement and cause of annoyance should arise.' In fact, he kept on making objections.

Hamida's mother 'caressed the idea,' but the chief opposition came from Hamida herself; she was only fourteen while Humayun was thirty-three, an opium-eater and already much married. It is said too that she was already betrothed and was in love, possibly with Hindal; also she was bold, with a will of her own. The Emperor made a state visit to her mother and said: 'Send someone to call Hamida Banu Begam here,' but the young Begam only said: 'I have paid my duty. Why should I come again?'

'Another time his Majesty sent a courtier and said: "Go to Mirza Hindal, and tell him to send the Begam." Hindal told the man: "Whatever I may say, she will not come. Go yourself and tell her." When the nobleman went and spoke, the Begam replied: "I shall not come."'

For forty days the girl resisted but an emperor is an emperor. Humayun, too, had another reason for persisting; in one of his darkest moments of defeat he had had a dream. 'When his blessed heart was cast down,' Gulbadan, orthodox as she was, evidently saw God's providence in this. 'He fell asleep in a sad mood, and saw in a dream a venerable man, dressed in green from head to foot and carrying a staff, who said: "Be of good cheer; do not grieve," and gave his staff into the royal hand, saying: "The most high God will give you a son who shall be named Jalalu-d-din Muhammad Akbar." The Emperor asked: "What is your honourable name?" He answered: "The Terrible Elephant, Ahmad of Jam;" and added, "Your son will be of my lineage."'

As has been seen, Humayun was inveterately superstitious and it happened that Hamida Banu Begam was in the line of the Terrible Elephant, and, 'at mid-day on Monday,—September, 1541—his Majesty took the astrolabe into his own blessed hand and, having chosen a propitious hour, summoned a mir and ordered him to make fast the

marriage bond. He gave the mir two laks of ready money for the dower, and having stayed three days after the wedding, he set out and went by boat to join his army and the battle that was still being waged.' For the sake of peace, he gave the furious Hindal leave to go to Kandahar with his mother, where Kamran seized them and took them prisoner to Kabul; as for poor Hamida, she was to spend the next three years wandering in Sind while Humayun, suffering defeat after defeat, tried fruitlessly to raise money and men.

With him she made the terrible desert journey to Umarkot. Seven months gone with child, it was astonishing that she survived the journey. Humayun's men had been stupid enough in this Hindu State to slaughter cows for food—to the Hindus the cow is sacred—and the Raja of Jaisalmer ordered all the wells to be filled with sand so that for four days and nights men and beasts had no water. Yet now, in these desperate near delirium days another omen appeared; it really must have seemed like a miracle. Hamida had a longing, not just for water but, as many pregnant women have, for one particular thing—she longed for pomegranate juice. Pomegranates in the desert! But the forlorn army chanced to meet a merchant who happened to have in his bag 'one juicy pomegranate.' This miracle heartened Humayun more than his reverses had grieved him and, sure enough, as if fortune had turned for him, the Raja of Umarkot greeted him kindly, lent supplies and money and provided the shelter so urgently needed for Hamida—something Humayun never forgot, just as he did not forget his saviour the water-carrier.

Umarkot, a small oasis town in the surrounding desert, must have seemed like paradise to the decimated caravan in whose trail so many men and animals had died of thirst, but it was an especial paradise for Hamida. Humayun left her there, under the protection of the Raja while he went on with his weary battling; four days after, in the early hours of the morning, in fact, before his cockerel could wake him, on October 5th 1542, 'there was born his Imperial Majesty, the

درختهای انار هم هست کردا کرد حوض تمام سه پریکزار

بای عن باغ همین است در وقت زردشدن باغهاسیار

world's refuge and conqueror, Jalalu-d-din Muhammad Akbar,' the name Humayun had heard in his dream. 'The moon was in Leo. It was of very good omen that the birth was in a fixed Sign, and the astrologers said a child so born would be fortunate and long-lived.'

It seems likely that the miniatures in Gulbadan's translated book illustrating the birth of Akbar and the rejoicing are 'embroideries', painted long afterwards; even remembering the Mughal genius for conjuring up a feast out of almost nothing, when Akbar was born there was really absolutely nothing except for what the generous Raja lent or gave, that and a little bag of jewels Humayun kept hidden, and always on his person; besides, he himself was thirty miles away. There were certainly no dancing girls, musicians and distribution of largesse, though, as Gulbadan tells, there were astrologers. Jauhar, Humayun's ewer-bearer, wrote in his own Memoirs that when the chief and generals came to offer their congratulations to the Emperor, 'His Majesty asked Jauhar to bring him a single pod of musk; he then called for a china plate and, having broken the pod, distributed it among the principal persons, saying, "This is all the present I can afford to make you on the birth of my son, whose fame I trust will one day be expanded over all the world, as the perfume of this musk now fills this tent,"' a trust that came true, though Humayun did not live to see it. For Hamida herself the quiet little picture, in which she sits recovering, with just a few of her court ladies, while the baby is being handed over to his nurses is probably true; there are only two women musicians; a simple cradle waits. Outside the garden is still dark, but light is touching the little town above on the hill. The ladies are evidently rejoicing and the good news is being given out by the gateman.

How long it took to reach Kabul is not known, but Kamran's runners were swift. Gulbadan must often have done what she did as a little girl—paced the ramparts of the Citadel, straining her eyes to see that tiny cloud of dust that

The infant Akbar placed in the care of his nurses

meant a runner. She knew now all about the marriage—was not Hindal in Kabul? It seems unlikely she had met Hamida, but the news of a son born to the Empress would have rejoiced the Princess's sore heart. Certainly that heart would have understood the long ordeal of the fifteen-year-old mother but now the royal line had an heir and the succession should be safe in spite of uncles as wicked as any in a fairy tale—if the infant survived.

There was anxiety about that but Akbar must have been a lusty baby; when he was only five weeks old the Court was on the march again; Humayun was finally driven out of Sind with what was left of his army and, after more 'terrible wanderings,' by boat or on horseback or on foot, reached Afghanistan and Kabul where he had to endure the most hurtful insult yet from his two half-brothers. Kamran refused to let him stay anywhere near Kabul; it would have been too dangerous; the people were already rebellious under the cruelty of his rule and would have rallied to their own Emperor. When Humayun went on to Kandahar, Askari gave him a cold reception; he let the Emperor camp outside the walls but would not allow him into the city.

To Gulbadan, as to the other ladies, this must have been shaming, but there was one alleviation. Askari agreed to take charge of the baby, Akbar. It seems an extraordinary thing for an emperor to give his heir into the hands of his enemies who had betrayed him again and again, and Akbar was later to go to the even more dangerous Kabul, to Kamran who had a son of his own, and what would have been easier than to kill the royal infant, especially at that time when baby deaths were so common? Perhaps Humayun, in his child-like way, trusted to Timurid tradition; perhaps there was no choice. Gulbadan says the Emperor had to leave so hurriedly, 'there was not a chink of time to take him,' but this seems far-fetched; it is more likely that the baby was too travel-worn to risk the long, rough way to Persia where Humayun had decided to take refuge; it is more likely still that Khanzada had been at work.

That extraordinary 'beneficent lady', as the older women of the Court were called, had such an influence over her nephews, even the turbulent ones, that it was like a spell, a spell that Gulbadan was to inherit. At this moment Khanzada happened to be in Kabul, presumably on her way back from Kandahar where she had been sent by Humayun to ask Askari for help. Though that had been refused she seemed, at least, to have aroused better feelings in Askari, whose wife took charge of Akbar and 'treated him as her own.' It was Jauhar, the ewer-bearer, who took the tiny Prince to Askari.

Humayun left most of his Court as attendants for his infant heir, so that a mere forty-four people went with him to Persia and of these only two were women, Hamida, parted from her baby, and a lady-in-waiting, just one.

Humayun was in desperate straits; he had only two or three tents, cooking pots had been forgotten so that the men had to cook the only meat they had, repugnant horseflesh, in a soldier's helmet. Kamran was master of Kabul, Kandahar, Badakhshan, with Askari attached to him; Hindal was Kamran's prisoner in Kabul; Sher Shah was ruler of Hindustan, but Humayun's luck or 'fortune' prevailed. When the Shah of Persia, Shah Tahmasp, heard that this uninvited guest had reached his frontier, he remained 'sunk in thought'—it is possible that he too had had dreams of Hindustan. Then he said, 'The Emperor Humayun has come to our frontier by a perfidious revolution of the firmament, a firmament unpropitious and crooked of gait. The Lord...has led him here.' This was most diplomatic; if the stars, not Humayun's brothers or Sher Shah, were to blame, Shah Tahmasp could make up his mind later as to whom he would support. Meanwhile, 'he sent all sorts of people to give the Emperor honourable reception, nobles and grandees, low and high, great and small. All came to meet the Emperor... All came and embraced him, and escorted him with full honour and respect. As they drew near, the Shah...came riding to meet the Emperor. They embraced.' This must have been balm to Humayun; as Gulbadan goes on to say: 'The friendship and concord of those two high placed pashas was as close as two nut-kernels in one shell.'

As a matter of fact there were passionate differences which almost led to Humayun's expulsion; they were smoothed over by the Shah's sister—which again shows the strong influence of Muslim women—but the alliance was finally made only when Humayun agreed to accept the 93

Persian interpretation of Islam, and, ostensibly, become a Shia, even wearing the distinctive Shia cap, something so distasteful to Gulbadan, an orthodox Sunni, that she glosses over this fact and writes: 'Great unanimity and good feeling ensued, so that during his Majesty's stay in that country, the Shah often went to his quarters, and on days when he did not, the Emperor went to him.'

She tells how the Shah provided houses and tents, horses and camels, luxurious clothes and food, royal baths; even the roads were swept and watered before the Emperor and Empress everywhere they went. Humayun hunted eight times during his stay in Persia: 'each time trouble was taken for him and Hamida Banu Begam used to enjoy the sight from a camel or horse-litter. The Shah's sister used to ride on horseback . . .beside her and was especially kind to the young girl and was hospitable with [the giving of] all sorts of stuffs, embroidered and others to Hamida Banu Begam—as was incumbent and fitting,' Gulbadan ends with dignity.

They were taken to see the sights: 'his Majesty visited all the gardens and the flower-gardens, and the splendid buildings . . .and the grand structures of olden days.'

Humayun stayed a month in Herat as Babur had done, made a pilgrimage to the shrine of Hamida's ancestor, the Terrible Elephant Ahmad; he probably trod the Holy Carpet of Ardabil, woven in 1540 and now in the Victoria and Albert Museum in London, which seems to bring the Emperor closer in history; but more important for India, he became fascinated by the Persian craftsmen, especially the painters of the exquisite miniatures. In his enthusiasm Humayun was delighted when some of these followed him to Hindustan after he had regained his throne; they helped to found the Mughal school of miniature painting.

In return for the honour paid to him and the lavish hospitality, Humayun, from his little bag of precious jewels, gave Shah Tahmasp the most precious of all, his inimitable diamond, the Kohinoor, which paid four times over what the Shah had spent. The Shah made up his mind; the alliance was firm, and in 1545 word came to Kabul that Humayun was on his way back from Persia with the Shah's army behind him. 'The Shah despatched his own son, Mirza Murad, and khans and sultans and amirs with his Majesty to help him, together with good arms and tents, folding and audience tents...excellently wrought, and all sorts of the things necessary and fit for a king, from the mattress warehouse and the treasury and the workshops and kitchen and buttery.' What Gulbadan does not mention was that the 'own son' was only a few months old, and the unfortunate little Prince Murad died before the army reached Kandahar.

The excitement in Gulbadan, Khanzada, Dildar and, of course, Hindal, must have been intense, and particularly for the first two there was a further expectation; Kamran's immediate reaction to the news was to send for Akbar, but this was also a cause of anxiety because Kamran's clear intention was to hold Akbar as a hostage against his father. All the same, for the first time Gulbadan saw the Prince of whom she had thought so much.

The little Akbar made the winter journey through the difficulties of snow and ice in company with a half-sister, Bakhshi Banu. 'He was given into the care of Dearest Lady, Khanzada Begam,' writes Gulbadan. 'He was two and a half years old when she received him into her charge. She was very fond of him and used to kiss his hands and feet, and say: "They are the very hands and feet of my brother the Emperor Babur, and he is like him altogether."'

Abu'l Fazl writes that, when Kamran saw Akbar, he was 'confused and astonished at the sight of that lustrous forehead whence streamed the glory of eternal dominion and success,' but that did not prevent him from letting his own son, Ibrahim, fight Akbar for a toy drum; indeed, reflecting that Ibrahim was the elder of the two and apparently the stronger, he thought the fight might be a good omen for himself, but Akbar, 'in spite of his tender years,' grappled with Ibrahim, and 'so lifted him up and flung him on the ground that a cry burst forth from the assembly, "Bravo!"' 'This was the beginning,' says Abu'l Fazl, 'of the beating of the drum of victory and conquest.'

Khanzada did not have Akbar for long. She had to leave him; 'When Mirza Kamran was sure that the Emperor was approaching Kandahar, he went to Dearest Lady and wept, and was very humble, and said with countless pains: "Go— may your journey be safe—to Kandahar; [speak for me] to the Emperor and make peace between us."'

Khanzada travelled as fast as she could, but was too late to prevail; after taking Kandahar, Humayun pressed on to Kabul; Askari, too, had grown humble, admitted his offences and paid duty to the Emperor, so Humayun could leave Hamida safely in Kandahar—she had lately had her second child, a little princess, born just before leaving Persia and was still weak, but the Emperor took Khanzada with him. It was to be the last of this indomitable lady's constant journeys and intercessions. On the way 'Dearest Lady, Khanzada Begam...had three days' fever and died.'

For Gulbadan it was a loss as sad, or perhaps sadder than Babur's; since childhood 'Dearest Lady' had been her guide and pattern. It is probable that Khanzada had the proud bearing, the beautiful and aristocratic features of her brother and perhaps the same wise, all-seeing brown eyes, the capable hands and the courage and hardihood; that she also had tact is plain but she was worn out with travel, continual efforts of counselling, restraining, reconciling. She had lived through personal tragedy: the shame of being given to Shaibani Khan; the deaths of her mother and the brother she adored, of her second husband and her last son, the only child she had been able to keep; she had known extraordinary poverty and equally extraordinary riches, and yet remained 'the Smiling One,' 'the Ever Beneficent Lady.'

> 'O soul at peace, return unto thy Lord,
>   well-pleased, well-pleasing!
> Enter thou among My servants!
> Enter thou My Paradise!'

These lines from the Quran must have comforted Gulbadan; if ever words were certain these were of Khanzada. She was buried at first in the mountain village where she died, but three months later her body was brought to Kabul and laid in the same burial place as Babur. What more fitting place for her than the Garden of Fidelity?

* * *

Mirza Askari with his sword slung round his neck

Humayun took Kabul: 'The victorious Emperor dismounted in triumph . . . when five hours of the night of Ramzan 12th had passed . . .'—this was almost certainly the hour fixed by the astrologers as prosperous and endowed with safety and good luck—'he entered the city with drums beating.' It was November, 1545 and on the 12th of the same month, Gulbadan recounts, 'her Highness, my mother, Dildar Begam and Gulchihra Begam, and this Lowly Person paid our duty to the Emperor. For five years we had been shut out and cut off from this pleasure so now, when we were freed from the moil and pain of separation, we were lifted up by our happiness in meeting this Lord of Beneficence again. Merely to look at him eased the sorrow-stricken heart and purged the blear-eyed vision. Again and again we joyfully made the prostration of thanks. There were many festive gatherings, and people sat from evening to dawn, and players and singers made continuous music. Many amusing games, full of fun, were played . . .'

Humayun as usual was generous: 'To widows and orphans, and kinsfolk of men who had been wounded and killed or who were in the royal service during those difficult days, he gave pensions, and rations, and water, and land, and servants. Great tranquillity and happiness befell soldiers and peasants. They lived without care, and put up many an ardent prayer for his long life. A few days later he sent persons to bring Hamida Banu Begam from Kandahar.'

Hamida came bringing her new little daughter. Humayun wanted to see if Akbar, whom his mother had been forced to leave when he was fourteen months old, would remember her now. The little Prince was brought in where all the ladies were seated, Hamida only one among many of them, but he at once ran to his mother. Abu'l Fazl puts it rather differently. 'By light divine . . . this firstling of Life's rose-bush . . . without difficulty, hesitation or mistake, and in virtue of his abiding intelligence, took refuge with his saintly mother.'

Gulbadan does not write of this though she must have been there; perhaps for her it was overlaid by the great feast for Akbar's circumcision, always of first importance in Muslim life. 'Muhammad Akbar was five years old when they made the circumcision feast in Kabul. They gave it in the large Audience Hall Garden. They decorated all the bazaars...the sultans and amirs decorated their quarters beautifully, and the begams and ladies made theirs quite wonderful in a new fashion. All the people were dressed in green.' Green was the Prophet's colour.

'The sultans and amirs brought gifts to the Audience Hall Garden. There were many elegant festivities and grand entertainments, and costly robes of honour and head-to-foot dresses were bestowed. Peasants and preachers, the pious, the poor and the needy, noble and plebeian, low and high— everybody lived in peace and comfort, passing the days in amusement and the nights in talk,' but the fighting was not over yet.

Humayun, with his usual lack of acumen, soon left Kabul to fight lesser battles in the north instead of pressing on or even establishing himself firmly in the lands around the city, and then, as Gulbadan puts it, 'illness attacked his blessed frame.' He was unconscious for four days and it was two months before he was well enough to move, and meanwhile Kamran seized his chance and retook Kabul.

It is here that Gulbadan, left in Kabul, herself gives for the first time in her book, the name of her husband.

Khizr Khwaja Khan seems to have been something of a turncoat; after deserting to Kamran, and going with him to Kabul, he went on to Askari in Kandahar; when Humayun was at last able to set about reconquering these territories and seemed likely to win, the Khan let himself down from the walls of the town and managing to reach the Emperor, implored forgiveness which, of course, Humayun gave—perhaps for Gulbadan's sake.

Now Kamran ordered her to write to Khizr Khwaja Khan: 'Tell him to come and join me and to keep an easy mind, for just as Mirza Askari and Mirza Hindal are my brothers, so is he. Now is the time to help,' but Gulbadan was not to be persuaded. One reason was Kamran's worse ill-treatment of the other royal ladies. As soon as he retook Kabul his men had gone into the haram and plundered and destroyed innumerable things. 'He put the great Begams into Mirza Askari's house,' Gulbadan wrote, shocked, 'and there he shut up a room with bricks and plaster and dung-cakes, and used to give the ladies water and food from over the four walls. He behaved very ill indeed to the wives and families of the officers who had left him for the Emperor, ransacking and plundering all their houses and putting each family into somebody's custody,' and Gulbadan refused to write to her husband; instead she temporised with something of Khanzada's tact. 'I answered: "But Khizr Khwaja Khan has no way of recognising a letter from me. I have never written to him myself. If he writes to me when he is away, [I answer] by the tongue of his sons. Write yourself what is in your mind."' At last Mirza Kamran sent some of his followers to fetch the Khan, but Gulbadan now dared to interfere and wrote to the Khan: '"Your brothers may still be with Mirza Kamran, [but] God forbid that you should have the thought of going to him and joining them. Beware, a thousand times beware of thinking of separating yourself from the Emperor." Praise be to God! the Khan kept to what I said.'

Humayun, though, had this time to blockade the Citadel for seven months; the ladies could see his camp from the high walls. 'We saw from above how he went out with his drums beating and we wept.' Then Kamran did something atrocious. 'It happened one day that Mirza Kamran went from his own quarters to the roof [of the Citadel] and that someone fired a gun from the camp. He ran and took himself off. Then he gave this order about the Emperor Akbar: "Bring him and put him in front."'

To Timurid thinking this was the ultimate blasphemy and should have been ultimate for Kamran. Someone warned the Emperor and, knowing his son was there in direct fire from the cannons, he could not fire a gun, but the people of Kabul had had enough of Kamran, his atrocities and murders, and soon the gates of the city were opened and Kamran capitulated.

Even after this, Humayun forgave him. There was a quality of the saint in this strange man; only once in his life did he do something mean and that was when, as a boy, after the battle of Khanua, he had gone on to Delhi, broken open the treasury and stolen all its wealth. That had particularly wounded Babur as he had just given Humayun the Kohinoor, but Humayun never broke his promises, and he had promised to do what Babur had asked him: 'Do nothing against your brothers no matter what they deserve.' Now he called them in assembly; all four sat on one carpet and all ate at one table, the highest possible honour, and Gulbadan was the only woman to be there. 'His Majesty graciously remembered this Lowly Person, and said to his brothers: "Gulbadan Begam used to say in Lahore: 'I wish I could see all my brothers together!' Her words have occurred to my mind, so let it be the will of the most high God... It lies not in my heart's depths to seek any Musalman's ill; how then should I seek the hurt of my brothers? May God grant to you all divine and beneficent guidance, so that our agreement and concord may endure!"'

Gulbadan goes on: 'There was wonderful cheerfulness and happiness [in Kabul] because many officers and their followers met their relations again, for they too had been sundered because of their masters' quarrels. Now they passed their time in complete happiness,' and, once again, Humayun lingered. 'The Emperor spent a year and a half in Kabul and then resolved to go south to the gentler climate of Balkh. He took up his quarters in the Heart-Expanding Garden, and his own residence was over against the lower part of the garden, and the Begams were...close by.'

There was even a picnic—perhaps the first expedition of pleasure the ladies had taken since leaving Agra.

'The Begams said to the Emperor over and over again: "Oh, how the riwaj will be coming up!"' Riwaj is a kind of wild rhubarb eaten in spring for toning the stomach and improving appetite. The Emperor took the hint and the haram cavalcade set out. 'It was a moonlit night so on the way we talked and told stories and the reciters, including Sarv Qad, the Straight Cypress, sang softly, softly.' Perhaps it was one of the songs the Emperor had brought back from Persia:

> Have you heard that sugar has become cheap in
> the town?
> Have you heard that winter has vanished and summer
> is here?
> Have you heard that basil and carnation in
> the garden are
> laughing surreptitiously because affairs have
> become easy?

Have you heard that the nightingale has returned from his
 travels, joined in the concert and become the master of all the birds?
Have you heard that now in the garden the branches of the
 trees have heard glad news of the rose, and shake their hands?
Have you heard that the soul has become drunk from the cup of spring?

When they reached the picnic spot the ladies' pavilions and tents had not arrived but Humayun's was set up, a tent with twelve divisions, each with a sign of the Zodiac and each sign had a lattice through which the light of the stars shone, 'and we all, his Majesty and all of us, and Hamida Banu Begam sat in that tent till three hours past midnight and then we went to sleep where we were, in company with that altar of truth [Humayun].'

In the morning there was a slight tiff which shows how difficult it was to live with an emperor, and, incidentally, how quickly Gulbadan had stepped into the shoes or, rather, the embroidered slippers, of Khanzada. The Begams, perhaps naturally, were late in getting up and, when the Emperor gave the order 'Mount,' they were not there. 'Go,' he ordered Gulbadan, 'and fetch them quickly,' but they were so long putting on their head-to-foot dresses that Humayun lost patience. 'What trouble waiting gives!' 'I was gathering them all together,' writes the Princess, 'and bringing them when he came to meet me and said: "Gulbadan! the proper hour for starting has gone by. It would be hot the whole way. God willing, we will go after offering the afternoon prayer." He seated himself in a tent with Hamida Banu Begam...but some vexation [still] showed itself in his blessed countenance and he was pleased to say: "All of you go on, and I will follow when I have taken some opium and got over my annoyance."

An encampment by moonlight

He joined us when, as he ordered, we had gone on a little. The look of vexation was entirely laid aside and he came with a happy and beautiful look in his face,' and the picnic ended in pleasure.

'Everywhere...the riwaj had put up its leaves. We went to the skirts of the hills and when it was evening, we walked about. Tents and pavilions were pitched on the spot and there his Majesty came and stayed. Here too we passed the nights together in sociable talk, and were all in company of that altar of truth,' but such days were rare.

Sher Shah had died and Humayun took the opportunity of regaining his empire and marched to Hindustan. At once Kamran broke the peace pact and, for the next eight years, was a menace in the north. Twice more he took Kabul and twice more Humayun, strong now, had to drive him out. In one of these battles Hindal was killed.

Hindal had been given what Humayun would have called 'an omen.' The story is told by the ewer-bearer, Jauhar. The Prince was riding with the Emperor and his train back to camp when three antelope passed by them: 'A retainer shot one, the second escaped but Mirza Hindal transfixed with an arrow the third; it fell on its side, raised its large eyes to heaven and expired. The attendants were astonished by its motions and said, "This antelope appears to have laid its complaint before the Redeemer of All Wrongs."'

Hindal was killed not by an arrow but a sword, trying single-handed to defend, from Kamran's men, one of the most humble of his servants, a clerk of the scullery. The Prince, perhaps the finest of all Babur's sons, was only thirty-three; he was Gulbadan's full brother and she gave her anger against Kamran full vent.

'I do not know what pitiless oppressor slew that harmless youth with his tyrant sword! Would to Heaven that merciless sword had touched my heart and eyes, or Saadat Yar, my son's, or Khizr Khwaja Khan's,' which shows again how she revered and loved the royal line even better than husband or

غالبا نیله کاو می کنند اند دو شاخ خورد ی دارد در کلوی و

child. 'All may be said in a word,' she wrote. 'Mirza Hindal gave his life freely for his sovereign, and, if it had not been for that slayer of a brother, that monster Kamran, calamity would not have descended from the heavens.'

His Majesty sent the news in letters to Kabul, and the city at once became like one house of mourning. 'Doors and walls wept and bewailed the death of the martyred Mirza.' His body was taken to the Garden of Fidelity and laid at Babur's feet.

At last, in 1552, Kamran was captured; this time there was no mercy. 'To be brief,' writes Gulbadan, in restrained coolness, 'all the assembled khans and sultans, and high and low, and plebeian and noble, and soldiers and the rest who all bore the mark of Mirza Kamran's hand, with one voice represented to his Majesty: "Brotherly custom has nothing to do with ruling and reigning. If you wish to act as a brother, abandon the throne. If you wish to be king, put aside brotherly sentiment . . . This is no brother! This is your Majesty's foe!"'

Humayun still would not kill a brother but even he had had enough. Already he had kept Askari in chains, then sent him to Mecca, equivalent to banishment; now he issued an order. 'Blind Mirza Kamran in both eyes.'

Gulbadan's manuscript breaks off here; perhaps the rest was simply lost or, perhaps, family feeling awoke and she could not bear to describe what happened. After all, Kamran personally had always been kind to her, showing her true affection, and no one, in history, has ever heard Kamran's side—there is no book of his, no Kamran-nama; if there had been, for all his cruelties and treachery he might have been easier to understand. What happened to him now was worse than death.

As usual Humayun left it to Jauhar to carry out the sentence and it is Jauhar who describes it: 'After receiving this command, we [the ewer-bearer and some officers] represented to Mirza Kamran in a respectful and a condoling manner that we had received positive orders to blind him: the Prince replied, "I would rather you would at once kill me;" I said, "We dare not exceed our orders." We then twisted a handkerchief up as a ball for thrusting into the mouth, and seizing the Prince by the hands, pulled him out of the tent, laid him down and thrust a lancet into his eyes (such was the will of God). This we repeated at least fifty times; but he bore the torture in a manly manner, and did not utter a single groan, except when one of the men who was sitting on his knees pressed him; he then said, "Why do you sit upon my knees? What is the use of adding to my pain?" This was all he said, and acted with great courage, till we squeezed some lemon juice and salt into the sockets of his eyes; he then could not forbear, and called out, "O Lord, O Lord, my God, whatever sins I may have committed have been amply punished in this world, have compassion on me in the next."'

He, too, was allowed to go to Mecca and with him, in the face of great opposition from her father, went the most devoted of his wives, Mah Chuchak, who looked after the broken Prince until his death and only survived him for seven months. She is held up in Muslim tradition as a pattern of faithfulness.

At last, free of his brothers, Humayun was able to reconquer Hindustan. Sher Shah's sons were no match for his great army and in July 1555 he reached Delhi and took the throne; the short-lived dynasty of Sher Shah was over. The Emperor made his palace in the Fort, in what is now called the Purana Qila, the Old Fort; it is ironic that, though, years ago, he had laid the foundation stone of what was to be a vast new capital, the only building of all the ones he had dreamed of was this, built by Sher Shah.

All the same, his 'fortune' had come full circle; indeed, the names he had encountered on that walk as a ten-year-old boy, Desire, Well-Being and Triumph seemed to have been fulfilled. Just one year later he spent 'a satisfying day,' something uncommon of late even for poor self-indulgent Humayun. Old friends had come back from Mecca and brought news of seemingly reformed brothers, which comforted him; letters had arrived from the royal ladies left in Kabul, including Hamida. Akbar had accompanied his father and was now in the Punjab, learning to be a prince under the tutelage of Humayun's most trusted general, Bairam Khan. All seemed at peace. Humayun had gone up to the roof of the tower he used as a library and 'shown himself to the people,' as was the duty of an emperor. Then he had 'interested himself in astrology, especially the rising of the planet Venus,' probably to find some auspicious date.

This roof is reached by two narrow flights of stone steps; the Emperor had started down them when, from the Fort mosque, the muezzin gave the call to prayer. Humayun tried to kneel, caught his foot in his long coat, and fell from the top to the bottom of the steps. Three days later he died.

* * *

Humayun's tomb is at Delhi; its dome was the first to be built in India in the gracious Persian style but is tiled in the blue that has come to be known as 'Delhi blue,' though it was used long before in Samarkand. The tomb was built after his death, not by Hamida, but Haji Begam, his older widow.

During the building she camped in the grounds to make sure everything was right. Gulbadan, when she came back to Hindustan, must often have visited her there.

The blue of that wonderful dome still rises into the Delhi sky and, inside the tomb, there is deep, abiding calm, as if Humayun, whom Gulbadan loved best of all her emperors, had at last found peace.

Courtyard with roof pavilion and stone steps

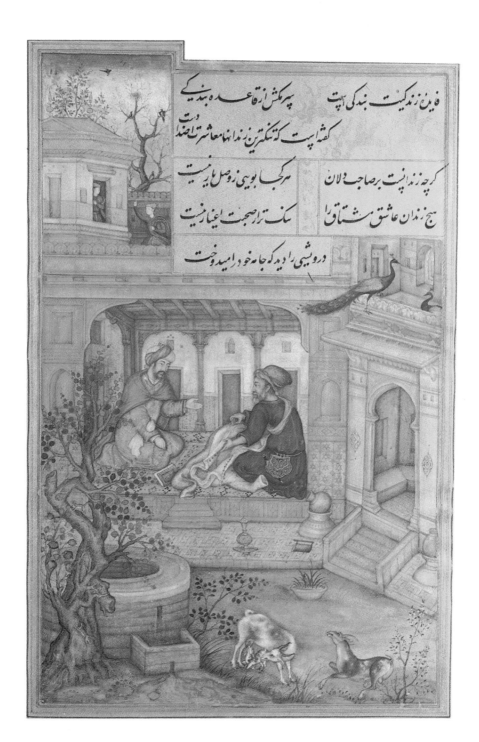

فی این زندگیست بندگی اپت پس کمش از قاعده بندگی کے

کشته است که تنگ ترین زندانها معاشرت اضداد وست

گرچه زندانست بر صاحب دلان هرکجا بویی ز وصل یار نیست

هیچ زندان عاشق مشتاق را سخت تر از صحبت اغیار نیست

درویشی را دید که جامه خود را امید دوخت

IV

Under Akbar

Gulbadan came back to India in the second year of Akbar's reign.

It must have been grievous to the royal ladies of the haram that none of them had been with Humayun at the time of his death, able to ease and strengthen him during the last days of suffering, though he may have been unconscious but, after the remorse and shame of Chausa when so many women and children had been lost, particularly his own small Princess Aqiqa, Humayun had vowed he would never take women into battle again—the taking of Hamida and Khanzada and their ladies into the troubles of Sind had been forced on him. Akbar, though, was with him in the campaign and, probably for the boy's safety, Humayun had kept the Prince with him most of the time but, sadly, in the month of the tragedy, Akbar had been sent to fight his first independent battle in the Punjab under Bairam Khan—one of the few sensible things Humayun did was to put his heir under the guardianship of this wise and loyal man.

Bairam had no easy task; Khanzada had been right: Akbar was in many ways another Babur. He refused any kind of teaching except in the prowess needed for sport or war; in his childhood days in Kabul when the astrologers found the auspicious hour for the little Prince to begin lessons, the royal pupil—'God's scholar,' Abu'l Fazl mistakenly calls him—was nowhere to be found; he had gone sporting. Hunting, pigeon-flying, polo were his favourite sports and, in a gentler mood, he was to play hide-and-seek with his ladies and backgammon on the great black and white chequered marble court at Fathpur Sikri with boy and girl dancers as live 'pieces.'

The young Akbar learning to shoot

پیش استادان دانا ور زنش آن روش که دو باشد چون شرف ملازمت این دقیقه یاب نکته دان عمر بر رسیده خود از دین
فزونی دانش بر کم کرده و در مقام حیرت می آید

و بنا خاطر رسیده که همانا او قت آنحضرت بغیر از کار صرف پسند باشد و باز میگوید که حین بهار عظیم یا نوا در فوذ و نو سیت
خداد اور از بدایع امکه و مشارب مختلفه و مدارج متنوعه در یک مجلس میفرماید که طبع جهان آرا و شوار رنی آید که حکام و علما
و فضلا و صنعت کران و دیگر الجاح و صلا و فامی کنت که بغیر روشن خ و زبان صحت و از مان فت یافت بلند و این جو حصلا فخ

The thirteen-year-old boy, dressed in a dark robe and a tiara, was crowned Emperor on February 14th, 1556, in a garden in the Punjab, but he did not have a throne; there were other and strong contenders for that. A descendant of the dreaded Sher Shah had immediately seized Delhi; Kabul was surrounded by the army of a rebel cousin, and there were riots in the Punjab, but Bairam remained cool. Under his advice Akbar quelled the riots first and so established his Punjabi domain; other advisers then pressed him to rescue Kabul but the Prince and Khan consulted together; it was a choice between a small kingdom in Kabul or an empire in Hindustan. They chose Hindustan.

Akbar had the courage of Babur too. As a child he had terrified his nurses and guards by insisting on riding fierce camels; he had once faced a tiger on foot and, in a skirmish, driven his war elephant through the wall of a house where bandits were entrenched, getting five arrows in his shield; now, to gain Hindustan, he had to face not only the scion of Sher Shah but a new enemy, an upstart Hindu, Hemu, who, though he had begun life as an ordinary merchant, was now calling himself Raja Hemu and was a skilled general, so skilled that unwittingly he did some of Akbar's work for him, driving the new Shah out of Delhi and proclaiming himself as ruler there. Hemu had a vast army but Akbar, with Bairam Khan, advanced against him.

The two armies met at Panipat, the very battlefield where, only thirty years before Babur had shattered the house of Lodi.

Hemu had gone into battle on his favourite elephant Hawai—the Rocket—but, as he sat in the howdah, he was wounded in the eye by an arrow which pierced through to his head and he fell back insensible. Hawai ran amok and Hemu's army, seeing their leader as it seemed dead, scattered too. The elephant was captured—its driver, not being armed, could offer no defence—and Hemu, still unconscious, was brought before Akbar.

The capture of Hemu at Panipat

Bairam said to the young King, 'This is your first battle. Prove your sword on this infidel; it will be a deed of great merit,' as it would certainly have been to Muslim thinking; but Akbar had something of Humayun's clemency in him as well as Babur's quixotic chivalry—it is told that once, when Babur could have fallen on an enemy by night, he sent a messenger to warn him so that the warrior would not be taken unawares—and now Akbar said, '[Hemu] is no better than a dead man. How can I strike him? If he had strength and sense I would try my sword,' meaning he would fight him, and Bairam had to decapitate the prisoner himself.

Hemu's body was sent to Delhi to be hung on a gibbet as a warning to rebels, but his head went to Kabul. This grisly message was not uncommon—heads were often laid at a victor's feet and there were those 'towers' of severed heads built after every battle; gruesome, gory and stinking as was Hemu's, it gave the ladies in Kabul relief and delight because it brought a double message: first that their boy Emperor had routed his rivals and won his throne, and also that it was safe now for the haram to come to Hindustan and join him, either in Delhi or Agra.

'The drums of joy beat high and, after thanksgiving and rejoicing, the expedition set out.' Hamida, as Empress Dowager, was chief, but next her in honour was Gulbadan as perhaps Babur's last surviving child—it is not certain if the 'Rosy-Cheeked Princess' mentioned was Gulbadan's sister or a niece.

Sarv Qad, the reciter, was there and probably sang the same songs on the way as she had done when Gulbadan was a child. For Gulbadan, as with Akbar at Panipat, it was history repeating itself: the elaborate packing up, the farewells, but now, for her, instead of sheer excitement, there would also have been regret. She knew that Akbar would be a very different emperor from Humayun; Akbar was strong, resolute and it was unlikely that the Court would be chivied from Agra or Delhi again, so for the Princess this could be hardly other than a lasting farewell to the mountain ringed city she loved.

'How can anyone like me fail to hold the delight of Kabul in his heart?' Babur had asked all those years ago and she, Gulbadan, was very like Babur. '... The castle above the river. The meadows shadowed at evening beneath the far snow summits, the blossoming trees...' but, regrets or not, Gulbadan had learned to be another Khanzada, a 'Smiling One,' and not let her grief spoil Hamida's joy.

The two had become as close as sisters; in camp their tents were pitched side by side; in the city, Gulbadan's house was next door. As they grew older Hamida, as the mother of the Emperor, became 'the Magnificent Lady,' Gulbadan 'the Beneficent' among the women of the Court; together they had now to meet many things that were to distress and worry them.

Possibly the first thing Akbar did, though innocently, that estranged them, was to send his one-time nurse, Maham Anaga—another Maham—to meet them. To be wet nurse to the heir of an emperor was a diplomatic, not a domestic appointment, because all of her children would become 'milk' brothers and sisters to the Prince, with special privileges

Maham Anaga

این جشن دل افروز مردهٔ نوروزی خاص میشد مواد بهجت وخوی خاص عام جهانیکیشت

and immunities, so that noblewomen vied for this office and great was the chagrin of those whose own babies came too late or early to provide the necessary milk. Maham was Akbar's chief nurse; there is a story too that when Kamran exposed the royal boy on the ramparts of Kabul, Maham Anaga shielded him with her own body. Akbar was devoted to her and Maham's influence over him was potent, far more so than Hamida's. Obviously she and Gulbadan regarded Maham Anaga as baneful and intrusive, and also it was impertinent of Akbar to send someone not royal to receive them.

However he soon came himself; though he was in the midst of fighting he rode a day's journey to meet them and Hamida's 'wishful eyes were gratified by the world adorning beauty of His Majesty, the Shahinshah.'

Akbar had risen higher than Padshah, just as the caravan of his haram which, after a short while in camp at Lahore, made its way to Delhi, had grown to great elaboration and splendour from the simple horse litters and palanquins that had brought Gulbadan with Maham from Kabul. With each reign the splendour increased. There is a description of a haram on the move in the time of Akbar's daughter-in-law, Nur Jahan, but his own must have been much the same. 'They travelled, a retinue of ladies surrounded by eunuchs, and women guards, under the escort of a prominent noble-man and his soldiers, making a long procession. Tartar and Kashmiri female slaves, fantastically dressed in burqas and riding handsome pad horses, marched in their wake, followed by three pairs of elephants carrying closed howdahs, in which the ladies-in-waiting sat. Behind the litters came the palanquins covered with rich cloth and network of gold, some ornamented with precious stones, others decorated with looking glass. Eunuchs, who marched very close to the caravan, drove away flies with peacock feathers stuck into the handles of enamelled gold work adorned with precious stones. Men guards holding sticks of silver and gold, went ahead shouting "Out of the way! Out of the way!"

A lady with serving girls behind a screen

'The path was sprinkled with water so that the dust might lie. They marched in great leisure and very slowly.'

Gulbadan was used to display—those feasts of Humayun, the marriage of Hindal—but Hamida was not; for her there had only been a taste of the magnificence of Persia; nor did this extravagance seem to fit with Gulbadan's idea of herself as 'lowly,' but it was for the royal dignity and it must be remembered that she was always 'behind the screen,' as many Muslim women, even nowadays, prefer to be; even when the ladies rode on an elephant the beast was taken into a tent and the driver covered his head with a thick cloth so that he would not see them as they climbed into their howdah.

Khizr Khwaja Khan, Gulbadan's husband, had been appointed by Akbar as Governor of Lahore, but there seems to have been no question of her leaving the Court to join him as there were rebellions in the Punjab; in fact, Khizr Khwaja was defeated and recalled. He is mentioned again as giving horses to Akbar and was with the Emperor when Akbar was hurt in a foray—it was the Khan who bound up the wound—but after this episode there is no further word about him and little of Gulbadan either until she made the pilgrimage of the Haj, but that span of her middle age spent quietly as a wife, widow, mother, grandmother was still woven closely with the Court.

She must, for instance, have shared the general grief and dismay when the insatiable ambition of Maham Anaga persuaded Akbar to dismiss his faithful tutor and regent, 117

General Bairam. True, Bairam Khan was honourably 'sent to Mecca,' but he was murdered on the way there—not, history is glad to know, by Akbar's orders.

For the moment Maham Anaga seemed triumphant, but not for long. Babur had openly and violently resisted any sort of control—'Who can bear the tone of authority?'—while all his life Akbar would appear to be manipulated, guided, cajoled, then suddenly the emperor in him would rise up and quench the interferer in no uncertain manner. Maham Anaga had forgotten that her affectionate little prince was now a man and far beyond and above her. Akbar had given a great deal of licence to her sons but now the youngest, Adham, behaved so abominably that, catching him daring to go into the imperial haram itself—an unpardonable trespass—the Emperor had him thrown down its marble stairs and, when that did not kill him, thrown down a second time. Adham died and Maham Anaga, disgraced and disillusioned, only survived him for forty days. Her spell was broken. Hamida and Gulbadan could not be sorry but these were not the only traits that grieved and shocked them in this, their greatly changed son and nephew.

For one thing they did not understand his policies; Babur and Humayun had both fought the Rajputs, and certainly Gulbadan, if not Hamida, must have heard much of the Hindu pride and ferocity when the rajas met defeat. 'What is that?' the young Akbar had asked Bairam when a besieged Rajput fort had at last surrendered and the young Prince suddenly saw huge fires flaming, not without but inside the walls. 'That is the Jauhar,' Bairam had answered and added calmly, 'It is customary.' Customary but horrific, the ritual immolation by burning of the wives, women and children of the defeated Raja before he and his men came out to be massacred themselves. It was true that, being Hindu, therefore infidel, the women might not have been respected by Muslims, but where was the Timurid tradition of chivalry?

Akin to this horror was the idea of 'sati.' Gulbadan had

The immolation of Rajput women at Chitor

heard tales of more than one of her own ancestors, Timurid begams, who had fatally stabbed themselves rather than comply when they were 'given away' to their captors, but that was by their own choice and most, like Khanzada, had accepted their new life as God's providence; but that a wife, by honour and tradition, was bound to throw herself on her husband's pyre and be burnt with his corpse seemed barbarous, as indeed it was. Sometimes it was not one wife, but all wives and concubines, even child ones, who were forced on to the pyre; the gateways of some of the old Hindu palaces have poignant little hand-prints made in vermilion, perhaps in protest on the last march of these innocents to the flames.

Akbar, to his credit, put an end to this, making it unlawful, and when his order was defied and the wife of one of the rajas was actually being dragged to her death, royal troops rescued her and Akbar took her under his own protection; but before he could pass his anti-sati law he had had, of course, to defeat the rajas and his way of doing this was not by fighting them but by reconciliation, leaving these proud Hindus to govern their own states under his shield, visiting and being visited by them—making friends of 'infidels.' Worst of all, he even married the daughter of the Raja of Amber, Jodh Bai.

Gulbadan, it seems, had never had a co-wife, but Hamida had been obliged to endure at least three, though one was Haji Begam, mother of the little drowned Aqiqa, many years Hamida's senior, who became her dear friend; even after Hamida, Humayun fell in love again with a lowly born girl, another Mah Chuchak, who gave him two sons and four daughters; a co-wife was hard to live with but at least all these were Muslims. There had, of course, been Hindu dancing girls at Court, probably concubines, but this marriage with Jodh Bai was nikah, a permanent marriage as against the convenient mu'ta which allowed a good Muslim to enjoy a woman or girl for a short while and then put her away, she, of course, understanding this and being compensated. This was not only a convenience; it kept Muhammad's

rule of only four full wives at a time, but Akbar, as usual, made his own rules; his marriage to Jodh Bai was celebrated with full splendour. It is not said if Hamida and Gulbadan attended, probably not, but Jodh Bai was part of Akbar's policy and, after her, more and more daughters of Hindu rajas were offered and accepted; the haram must have been overflowing—and the Emperor even allowed his Hindu women to have a temple and to worship and practise their own rites in the haram itself, those up to now sacred precincts.

One raja though, the Rana of Mewar, never submitted to Mughal rule. When Akbar had besieged and conquered Mewar's high-walled, almost impregnable fort of Chitor, he found the Court and army had removed themselves over the mountains. The Rana reappeared years later at Udaipur where his descendants were to build the famous Lake Palace of Udaipur. It was at Chitor that Akbar, renowned for tolerance, did one of his unpredictable acts of cruelty; he ordered the massacre of thousands of Rajputs and the innocent peasants who had taken refuge under the walls.

There was a curiously sadistic trait in Akbar: Abu'l Fazl tells how he delighted in watching a spider catch, entangle and eat flies; how, when he discovered that frogs could kill sparrows by the froth they spewed out, he used to set them at one another, for which even Abu'l Fazl's fulsomeness could not find an excuse and so he wrote tactfully, 'Let us pass on to another subject.'

As Akbar grew older and the Empire more settled, hunting took the place of battles; it, too, was cruel. Hundreds of soldiers would surround some chosen miles of jungle and gradually beat inwards, driving the animals until they were in a vast net. The Emperor went in first to take his prey—no other word for it because the animals, though dangerous, were helpless. Then the nobles took their turn and, lastly, the common soldiers. Akbar hunted on a favourite elephant or horse, sometimes with a hawk, but his favourite way was with cheetahs, the small lithe Indian leopards.

A Hindu lady worshipping at a lingam

They were trapped in pits or nets and Akbar himself would often ride out to see them taken out blindfolded and put in strong wicker cages. Skilled keepers trained them and soon they could stalk and kill and bring the kill back. Akbar loved his cheetahs and personally oversaw their food; they were groomed, wore jewelled collars and were carried to the hunt blindfolded as a hawk is hooded, but sitting on precious carpets. One which jumped, with amazing courage, over a gorge to catch a deer and jumped back carrying it, was made 'Chief Cheetah,' and was entitled to have a drum beaten before it when it went out in the hunt procession.

This was the sport of emperors, extremely expensive and far flung, sometimes using as many as fifteen hundred men, but one day, after the tremendous 'beating in' had been done, Akbar suddenly showed his compassionate side: he ordered the nets to be lifted, the beaters, princes, nobles, huntsmen, cheetahs, hounds, all to withdraw, and the hunted beasts were allowed to go free.

There were in this strange man the same mystical yearnings that had beset Babur. Akbar would suddenly gallop his horse into the desert to be alone and no one dared interrupt him. After the fall of Chitor and, perhaps—who knows—in repentance for the massacre of the peasants afterwards, he had made a pilgrimage to the shrine of a Muslim saint who had founded an Order of holy men who were given the saint's name, Chishti. Akbar went there on foot which shows a sign of his repentance and, in this monastery shrine, he met the saintly man he was to honour above all others, Shaikh Salim Chishti.

Akbar had one great grief; for all his three hundred wives, and the five thousand women Abu'l Fazl describes as being in his haram, none had given him an heir. Twin sons had been born but had died almost at once; girl babies too had been born but no more boys. It was the same puzzle that had faced Babur and Humayun, but with Akbar more inexplicable; he was not absent so often, and there was no reason to doubt his potency; he may have thought it was a punish-

A cheetah hunt

ment for his own pride and turbulence, and so he made this pilgrimage, humbly and with good intent, and Shaikh Salim promised him that he would have three more sons.

Almost at once Jodh Bai, the Princess of Amber, became pregnant; to make certain of the prophecy, Akbar sent her to Shaikh Salim's house and, on August 10th, 1569, she had a son. The new little prince was called Salim after the Shaikh. When he became Emperor, Salim took the name Jahangir. Akbar insisted that both mother and child should stay with the Shaikh for another three months; history does not tell what were the feelings of a young Hindu wife, schooled in Rajput pride, at having to live in such proscribed Muslim holiness, but the court rejoicings were tremendous, though tempered for Hamida and Gulbadan by the fact that this future Emperor would be half Hindu and so half infidel.

As for the Chishtis themselves, they were of the most liberal sect of Islam, the Sufis; it could be said that the Shias were perhaps the most strict; and Sunnis, to which the Mughals, including Gulbadan, belonged, were orthodox, holding firmly to the teaching of the Prophet as set out in the Quran, and the Sufis far more tolerant—loosely so, Gulbadan would have thought. They 'interpreted' the Quran, not simply obeying it to the letter but taking a wider view of the Sharia, the way of the Prophet. To Akbar, Sufism gave scope to his growing awareness of the outer world, of the similarities of most religions, Hindu as well as Muslim, later Christian, Zoroastrian, Buddhist.

Two other sons were born under the same, to Akbar, miraculous protection of the Shaikh: Murad in 1570 and in 1572, Daniyal. The Emperor now had three fine sons and it was in gratitude to Shaikh Salim Chishti that, just twenty-three miles from Agra, Akbar built Fathpur Sikri, his fabulously beautiful city in which he held court for fourteen years, but which had eventually to be abandoned because the Emperor and his architects forgot one simple but necessary thing, water—strange, when the Mughals had such a passion for water, making wells, canals and the perfection of

marble pools, fountains and water channels in every garden and palace they designed.

Fathpur has been called a ghost town, given over to tangles of bougainvillea and oleander, to wild peacocks and parakeets, monkeys, perhaps cobras, yet to go there when it is empty of tourists and workmen, in the earliest morning or at night by moonlight, is to feel the throbbing life of a royal city evoked all around; it is, in fact, uncommonly alive, perhaps because the dry climate around Agra has so perfectly preserved the rosy stone of which it was built. It seems that the backgammon court is ready for play; that any moment there will be the roll of kettledrums announcing the entrance of the Emperor or that there will be the sound of a flute, or the nasal sing-song of a dancing girl. The stone tethering rings in the stables and elephant stalls seem waiting for their beasts. From Jodh Bai's pavilioned house, where the stone is carved into lattice like lace, it seems impossible that the Queen will not come out to take her bath in the bath-house; or that in the debating hall the voices that were heard sometimes all the night through should be silenced and that Akbar should not be sitting on his throne raised on the great central pillar with, in the galleries all round, scholars, poets, learned men of every nation and creed—even Christians—arguing and arguing.

In Sikri there is still Akbar's pigeon post office from which urgent messengers flew in and out and, towering over the houses, the mosque, in which the Shaikh's tomb seems small and lonely, for all the ornate marble with which Akbar's grandson, Shah Jahan, unfortunately covered it, in contrast to the intrinsic rose red stone of the mosque. The tomb is still a shrine; couples still come there to pray for the gift of a child, but as Akbar became greater, bringing almost the whole of India under his sceptre, he seems to have forgotten his reverence for the Shaikh. Again he had come under an influence, that of Abu'l Fazl who became his greatest friend and who, besides writing the Akbar-nama, Akbar's royal biography, wrote in seven years the extraordinary Ain-i-

کل در یکجا می شکفد از دو رمثل ملک کل کلانی سے نمایید بوته این

از بوته کلبن کلانترست کبیر سرخ طور بو یکی دارد خوش آیند است

Akbari, a complete study of everything to do with the Court and Emperor from day to day; it tells, in immense detail, how Akbar lived, how he ruled, fought, hunted, ate, worked, slept or played; for instance, how he played polo at night with balls made of palas wood that glowed in the dark. There are long accounts of his favourite elephants and their cost; of how Akbar disliked meat so that for months he would go without it but, when he consented to break his fast, the first dishes were always brought from his mother, Hamida's, house; how a boatload of ice was brought down the Jumna for the palace every day; how Akbar never drank anything but Ganges water, a Hindu custom, of which there were to be more and more.

It is certain that Hamida and Gulbadan deeply distrusted the influence of Abu'l Fazl and grew more and more dismayed. At Hindu festivals Akbar even wore the 'tilak,' the red forehead spot, mark of a Hindu who has fulfilled his rites. He altered the style of his turban to a Rajput one, adopted much of the Rajput style of dress, just as he tried to persuade the Muslim ladies of the haram to wear, for coolness sake, the short bodice, bare midriff and the light gauzy skirts and veil of Hindu women. The Timurid descended ladies indignantly refused and kept to the customs of their mothers and grandmothers, but it might indeed have been these, to her, grievous deviations of her revered Emperor that, in 1576, made Gulbadan decide to make the Haj.

She was presumably by then widowed or she could hardly have left her husband. She, and Hamida too, evidently lived outside the haram, but whether in Fathpur Sikri or in the Punjab, where they may have accompanied Akbar when he moved there for a while, or whether they stayed in Agra is not known. It is sure though that Gulbadan kept much of the state of her aunt Khanzada and, no matter where her home or palace may have been, it would have had staterooms, open verandahs and pillars with the customary and beautiful trellises carved of stone. The floors would have been spread with carpets and the rooms furnished with low daisis, or day-beds, on which big and heavy tasselled cushions for leaning against were set; there would have been the low tables and bookstands that can be seen in court miniatures. The air would have been scented, probably with ambergris or sandalwood or aloe wood in case the Emperor came— Akbar was fond of scent. Incense burners would have been lit at evening against insects and any possible vulgar food smells. Outside, on the steps, rows of pattens, or even slippers, may have been dropped so that the serving maids and eunuchs could come and go silently barefoot; and there would have been a garden of flowers, the brilliance of bougainvillea, of oleander, roses, the gentle blue of plumbago, in spring narcissi and, of course, a fountain splashing into a pool.

130   There were comings and goings: visits to and from

Hamida and from countless cousins and friends, long conversations accompanied by the swish of fans, children playing; perhaps sometimes the little princes paid visits to this august aunt and mixed with Gulbadan's own grandchildren, and every now and then, often unexpectedly, the Emperor came himself. That he was deeply fond of Gulbadan is plain from the fact that it took her a year or two to persuade him to let her go on the Haj.

Her life had always been ruled by her religion, and she deplored Akbar's ways; for her infidels were not for hobnobbing with, they were for slaying—did it not say so in the Quran? And was not one of Akbar's titles Ghazi, the Avenger of God? Of course, if any pagan repented and was converted he or she would be welcomed, but to encourage them in their own beliefs as Akbar was encouraging them, she, taught as she was by the Maulvis, was sure no true Muslim should accept, and Princess Rosebody decided to make the only protest that she could compass—the pilgrimage of the Haj.

* * *

Islam is a faith that, to outsiders, can seem harsh, narrow and the least mystical of all religions; its rules, certainly, are founded on common sense, but it is capable of the deepest interpretation, and for observance and prayer makes demands that many Christians, even the most devoted, would find difficulty in following; yet these are the daily responses for millions of every-day men and women.

There are five precepts or 'pillars' that uphold the faith.
The first is faith itself, summed up in, 'There is one God, Allah, and Muhammad is His prophet.'
The second is prayer, prayer of two kinds: one private and spontaneous, the other a set ritual offered five times a day.
The third pillar is the Haj, the pilgrimage to Mecca.
The fourth is 'fasting,' in particular for Ramzan, or Ramadan, when, in the ninth month of the Muslim year, the faithful must go without food or drink from sunrise to sunset, a terrible ordeal in hot weather, particularly the abstinence even from water; they must also not indulge in sex. The fast ends in the beautiful festival of Id, the rising of the new moon.
The fifth pillar is the giving of alms.

131

To a Muslim the Quran is the holy of holies. It must
never be put under other books, no one must drink or smoke
when it is being read and it must be listened to in silence. It
is also a classic of great beauty with a rhythm of peculiar
potency; the cadences fall with a calming effect, even if the
listener cannot understand the words:

> 'Praise belongs to God, Lord of the Worlds,
> The Compassionate, the Merciful,
> King of the Day of Judgement,
> 'Tis Thee we worship and Thee we ask for help.
> Guide us on the straight path,
> The path of those whom Thou hast favoured,
> Not the path of those who incur Thine anger
> nor of those who go astray.'

The call to prayer of the muezzin from the minaret of a
mosque is more eloquent than bells.

Women do not go to the mosque; they pray at home but
even there a ritual is observed. When a woman prays, her
veil has to cover her hair completely and is folded low down
on the forehead, going behind the ears and taken round to
hide her neck; this veil must be wide enough to fall to the feet
and the attitude of prayer is the same as the men's, standing,
not bowing, folding hands on breast as a sign of humility, in
fact, doing what the Prophet laid down: 'Pray with your body
as well as your heart.'

All this Gulbadan had observed with her whole heart
and soul since she was a child, and perhaps she hoped that
the hardship of the pilgrimage, her earnest prayers, and the
prayers of her companions, would make the great Emperor,
her beloved and revered nephew, pause and think of the
harm he, in her eyes, was doing to Islam. She was deter-
mined and at last he let her go, though reluctantly.

There were grave objections: Gulbadan Begam was already in her middle fifties, elderly for an oriental woman,
and Akbar knew the journey would bring more hardship

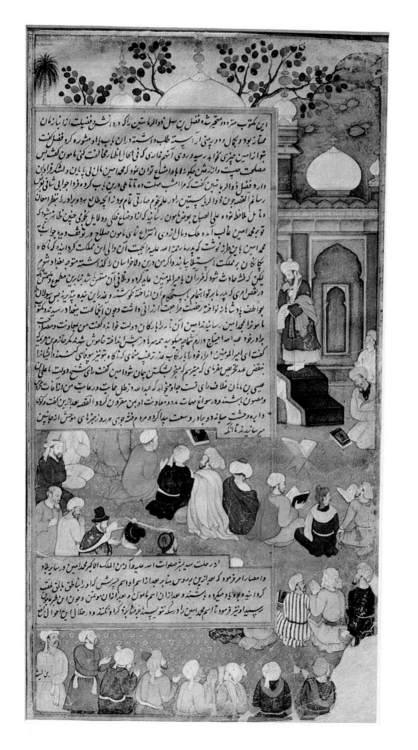

than even she could imagine, and not only hardship, danger, because the way led through Rajput country and Rajputs were unruly. It would too be a long absence, though how long neither of them dreamed. Akbar, though, had secretly always wanted to make the Haj himself, and so at last he let Gulbadan go, even walking the first stage with the caravan from Agra to Ajmer, wearing the seamless white dress of a pilgrim. He paid for the whole expedition from his own purse and, like the Shah of Persia in Humayun's day, sent one of his own sons to escort it. This was his second son, Murad; he was a little older than that first Persian Murad, not yet quite six years old; at Gulbadan's request he was 'excused from his duties,' and sent back to Agra.

Of the ladies who went with her some are already known in this story: there was Haji Begam, Humayun's senior widow who had built his tomb—her name 'Haji' seems to indicate that she had made the Haj before. Then there was Gulnar, Babur's Circassian slave, the Red Red Rose who must now have been truly elderly, as was the reciter, Sarv Qad, who would have sung for the pilgrims, not songs of spring or marching songs but hymns or sacred chants. The widow of Askari who had looked after Akbar as a baby came too, and there were some new names; for the first time Gulbadan's grand-daughter is mentioned, called, poor girl, Umm-Kulsum, Mother of Plumpness, and Akbar sent one of his own wives. The leader in charge of these important ladies was a sultan, appointed by the Emperor, and he took, among many other presents, twelve thousand dresses of honour, which gives an idea of the scale of the expedition—it was to need two boats to take it from Surat, the port from which at last the ladies embarked.

Travelling across Hindustan they were probably escorted from one garrisoned fort to another because there was always the danger of ambush and pillage. The dust and heat can be imagined, especially under the stifling head-to-foot dresses they wore if they rode. There would have been, too, flies and insects, lack of water, difficulties of food; meat gone putrid, little fruit—perhaps, like the prophet, they lived on dates; and there would have been illness—the old enemy dysentery and boils and fevers.

134   At Surat they were held waiting for a year, because their

'passes' were not in order; each pilgrim had to have a pass stamped with a picture of the Virgin Mary and the Infant Christ, this because the Portuguese were masters of the sea. The ships were Turkish transports, heavy sailing ships, with oarsmen for times when the wind dropped.

On the last stage of the journey, the pilgrims would have put on the white seamless wrapper, the same as Akbar had worn on the first march; the women had white veils and, from that moment of outer symbolism, each was in the inward state of holiness that comes from the wish of a heart and soul to draw near to Allah, God. Over and over again, from Jeddah to Mecca, they chanted 'Labbaika—Here I am, come to serve Thee.' It was as if the whole company of each ship was crying out and Gulbadan must have sensed even more deeply what she had always known, that she was part of something vast, wonderful, infinite, and truly had become that 'insignificant person' she liked to call herself, because now princesses, nobles, slaves, even the humble boatmen were all alike.

Once landed, she must have been filled with urgency and a most un-Gulbadan-like impatience as she made the last and longed-for march to Mecca itself.

The first impression of the Ka'ba, the House of God, as it is called, is one of enormity; it is a great windowless cube, traditionally said to have been built by Abraham and holding the black stone, perhaps a meteorite, said to have been given to Abraham by the Archangel Gabriel. The whole rises with a strange mystical power skywards, and at the same five times every day, millions of Muslims, all over the world, turn symbolically towards it in a great unison of prayer. Now Gulbadan and all her royal train came near enough to touch it, and at once the long months of hardships, dangers and interminable delays seemed a disregarded moment of time.

To fulfil the Haj the Ka'ba has first to be circled seven times but, for those who take the pilgrimage most seriously, there are preliminary washings: not just the ritual ablutions laid down by the faith, but for each pilgrim a cleansing and purifying of herself to be ready for the days that are coming. Then each goes to say her own prayers in the enclosed side of the Ka'ba, close by the holy 'house', each acutely aware that Muhammad himself had prayed here too. Gulbadan, like so

many others of the deeply devoted, must have felt her heart beating in time to that steady paean of praise and, like so many before and after her, wished she could stay in that holy place to the end of her days.

Yet the Haj had hardly begun. Next day there came the 'race,' again made seven times, between the sacred hill of Safa and the summit of Mount Marwa, a 'race' because it commemorated the desperate search for water by Hagar, Abraham's slave, when he cast her out into the desert with her little son, Ismail. The 'seven times' are strenuous enough to try a strong man, but of the hordes of people, rich and poor, old or young, well or ill, only the very old or badly crippled have to be helped or carried; most, even if they can only limp or shuffle, faithfully follow the Mu'allin who leads them in chanted prayers; it must have amazed the pampered ladies of the Mughal Court to find they had an endurance they did not know they possessed; nor did they mind the fierce sun and dust and heat on their delicate skins.

After these first solemn days of the Haj a pilgrim could, if he or she wanted, take a rest in return for the sacrifice of a lamb or goat, but it can be guessed that Gulbadan would have chosen, as most do, to spend this interlude in chant and meditation, keeping to the pilgrim simplicity of white, praying in steady tranquillity yet impatient for the moment when the pilgrimage would begin again. On the seventh day, as one mass, they rose to journey on foot to the other holy places beginning with the Day of Watering when they would provide themselves and their beasts with water for the desert journey to the valley of Arafat; they set out, all to the same goal, yet each curiously alone in her own world of ecstasy and expectation. Even for a princess little baggage would have been carried because things of the outer world had become of no importance, her needs infinitesimal; what frugal food was necessary could be bought for a few pence on the way because food-sellers followed the pilgrimage.

The Haj would rest for the night at Mina and after the next day's journey reach a small rocky hillock in the valley of Arafat to keep a vigil of prayer and listen to a sermon preached in memory of the last sermon given by Muhammad on that very hill. Often the words could not be heard because of the vastness of the valley but the multitude listened, thousands of men and women, faces upturned towards the scorching sun, lips chapped, often bleeding from dryness, often with tears pouring down their cheeks; they were oblivious now of discomfort, even suffering, because this was true religion, transcendent, living.

At sunset it was time to start back to Mecca; some pilgrims camped for the night but many, on the same tide of exaltation, went on to Mina for the ritual stoning of the devil, thousands of outstretched arms coming from an undulating mass of white as the people, thronged and crushed themselves together in almost hysterical fervour to throw the hail of stones against evil.

Next in the Haj comes what to western thought is hideous: the sacrifice, when thousands of sheep and goats are slaughtered in memory of Abraham's devotion, and obedience to God, even to the horror of offering up his own son, Isaac. The slaughter remembers too the ram caught in the thicket and killed in Isaac's place. It is a necessary part of the Haj but the begams would not have been expected to cut the throats of the animals themselves, a deputy would have done it; their presence though would have been necessary at this orgy of terror and blood. In contrast, cool, pure water was then drunk from the sacred spring of Zamsan, a well uncovered by Gabriel to rescue Hagar and Ismail from dying of thirst. Then, for a further three days, until the blood of the sacrifice had dried, the pilgrims should stay in Mecca, again washing and purifying themselves, the men having their hair shaved, the women washing and trimming theirs. Then there is a last circling of the Ka'ba with a chant and prayers, the huge block covered now with a cloth of black and gold and the Haj is over. It is said that not one soul comes away without finding new strength and resolution, even if it is only the strength—perhaps the greatest strength of all—acceptance of all life will now bring, no matter what that may be.

Gulbadan stayed in Arabia for three and a half years and made the Haj four times—the fairy-tale Princess Rosebody must have had the endurance, toughness and faith of a saint; Islam has its saints too, not of the haloed miracle-making kind, but holy men and women living apart and who often have the vision of prophecy as had Akbar's Chishti Shaikh Salim. In those years Gulbadan would have visited the Arabian shrines and particularly gone to Medina where Gabriel spoke to Muhammad and where the prophet started his real ministry.

Though the ship that eventually came to fetch the ladies was called Tezrah—the Swift—and its companion S'ai—Effort—they were misnamed; both were wrecked at Aden and it is difficult to imagine a more desolate place to be stranded in; even now, with its modern water tanks, bazaars,

ships constantly coming and going, it is arid, dull and burningly hot, but then there was nothing to alleviate its harshness, added to which the Turkish Governor was as inhospitable as he was rude; the unfortunate pilgrims were marooned there for months, partly because Akbar was away in Kabul and could not arrange a safe and large enough escort to fetch them.

It was March 1582 when, after this long absence, almost seven years, they finally reached Hindustan and Agra. On the last stages they had been heartened because every day an amir came from the Emperor with greetings, and when they paused to visit Ajmer, that shrine of the Chishtis, Prince Salim came, probably bringing Hamida, who must have so longed to go with them. Then at the next stop came the Emperor himself. 'The night of re-union was kept awake by questions and entrancing stories: gifts were showered and happiness brimmed over. The family was together again.'

How much Akbar reverenced these senior ladies and his senior wives is shown by his giving them control of the Uzek, the most important imperial seal—no royal document was valid without its mark but the reverence did not mean he honoured their beliefs, and what Gulbadan discovered on her return must have given her great grief; it seemed her four makings of the Haj, her prayers, had been in vain; the Emperor's errancy was worse, far worse, amounting almost to heresy—it is ironic that the very qualities for which history extols Akbar, his tolerance and width of thinking, were what was most abhorrent to his mother and his aunt.

In 1579 he had written to the—up to then detested—infidel Portuguese in Goa, asking them to send three learned men to his Court, so that he could learn about Christianity. Three Jesuits had come, nicknamed 'the Nazarene Sages,' and Akbar had paid them great honour, visiting the chapel they had been allowed to make and particularly the 'crib' set up at Christmas, even taking off his turban and laying it on the ground before the Infant Christ. Muhammad had acknowledged Christ but as one of the prophets, not as God,

The Jesuits in the Ibadat-Khanah (House of Worship)

not as the Son of God, and this taking off the turban was the greatest reverence a Muslim could give. Akbar had also appointed one of the Jesuits as tutor to his son, Mirza Murad, the same little prince Gulbadan had sent back from the Haj.

The Jesuits hoped to convert Akbar and, at one time, thought they had, but Akbar was still adept at escaping, as it were, 'from under,' and presently they left. This was when Hamida tried to show her dislike and distrust of them; the Fathers would accept no gifts and only enough money for the journey back to Goa, but their leader, Rudolpho Acquaviva, asked one favour. 'The great Hamida Banu Begam has among her house-slaves a Russian from Moscow, his Polish wife and their two sons, all Christians. We beg her to free them and let them come back with us to Goa and the Christian life.' Hamida indignantly refused until the Emperor, who thought nothing too good for his friends, insisted and she had to give them up.

This, though, was not the worst; though Abu'l Fazl's praise for the ladies was as fulsome as usual, they knew this man's power and his, to them, ignoble thoughts—worse than ignoble, blasphemous; but there had grown up between him and Akbar one of those friendships of mutual respect and sympathy that even his mother could not break. That it was pure there is no doubt; Akbar seems to have been the reverse of sensual. Most of the other Mughal emperors had, in their lives, one great love for a woman, each time for a wife: for Babur it was his Moon Lady, Maham: for Humayun, Hamida: for Jahangir, Nur Jahan who not only loved but ruled him: for Shah Jahan, Mumtaz Mahal, for whom he built the Taj, but Akbar seems not to have had a special love for any of his wives, though he paid them honour and liked their company. His early influences, Bairam and Maham Anaga, had been discarded, but Abu'l Fazl's ceased only with the courtier's death.

During Gulbadan's absence in Mecca, Akbar had issued a document, the famous Mahzar, the 'infallible decree' which declared that he, the Emperor, was not only the temporal

Abu'l Fazl presenting his book

guide of his subjects, but their spiritual leader and dictator as well, which, to Gulbadan and her like, was blasphemy indeed because it was against the fundamental belief of Islam in which the Quran stands above any human ordinance. He had taken the rank of Mujtahid, 'an infallible authority on all matters Islamic.' He had stopped the custom of sending alms to Mecca, no longer went on pilgrimage to the shrine of his once revered Chishtis at Ajmer, and even had the effrontery to preach in a mosque and to try and recite the Khutba there, including his new doctrine. Fortunately he was seized with such a fit of trembling that he could not go on. Hamida— and Gulbadan when she heard—must have trembled too; 'Beware of God's temper,' says the proverb, but Akbar seemed immune even when he did desecration, such as letting pigs, those unclean animals, into a mulla's garden.

He was also an emperor of a haughtiness even these ladies had not met before; Babur had never been as imperious —he was too sensitive to his sins; Humayun was hardly imperious enough, but with Akbar, though Hamida, as his mother, might have remonstrated, she only dared to do so gently and he obviously did not listen, while Gulbadan knew that if she had given vent to her feelings of outrage, she might have been sent back to Mecca, not of her own free will, but banished. It would not, though, have been fear that held her back—she was a true daughter of the Tiger—it was still that innate and unswerving reverence for the title 'Emperor' and of the blood royal. She could not help but esteem Akbar no matter what he did.

The esteem was certainly mutual and it was now, when she was well over sixty, that the Emperor gave his 'Order': 'Write down what you know...' and she began her book. Surprisingly, considering his truancies and deliberate ignorance as a boy, Akbar had grown up to have a real delight in books and philosophical debate and had such a memory that it seems none of the sages he was later to entice to his Court realised he was illiterate. He is said to have had more than twenty-four thousand books in his library, more still in the haram, and for him they were not mere possessions; every day he was read aloud to and when the reader stopped, 'His Majesty makes with his own pen a mark and rewards the readers with gold or silver according to the number of pages read out. Among books of renown there are few which are not read in his Majesty's hall.' He had the same passion for painting—the greatest art commission of his reign was for an illustrated copy of the Hamza-nama—Hamza, Muhammad's uncle, fascinated Akbar. For this work a team of a hundred painters, gilders and binders were employed; it runs to twelve volumes and originally had more than a thousand illustrations. Gulbadan must have gloried in it and, in this sphere, Abu'l Fazl's influence, even in her eyes, did nothing but good.

It was in this time that Abu'l Fazl too had his 'Order': it was for the Akbar-nama: 'Write with the pen of sincerity the account of the glorious events of Our dominion and increasing victories'—evidently Akbar had now caught his friend's flowery style. It is not surprising that in this plethora of art and writing Gulbadan's modest small account dropped out of sight.

Only two or three times more is she mentioned, but it is known that she travelled again. In 1589 Akbar had conquered Kashmir, that exquisite land of lakes, mountains and vales still called the Pearl of Hind. He was enchanted by it; his son Jahangir fell in love with it even more deeply and it was here, with his queen, Nur Jahan, that Jahangir was to make the famous Gardens of Nishat and Shalimar. Akbar was not such a lover of nature—he seems to have taken little interest in flowers and birds—yet even he lingered and sent for some of his own haram, but he also felt a longing for his mother and ordered that a petition should be written asking her to come. He added a verse dictated with his 'pearl laden tongue':

'The pilgrim may go to the Ka'ba to make the Haj
Oh God! May the Ka'ba come towards us.'

It was meant to be more than complimentary, but to Hamida and Gulbadan it was most irreverent. However, they set out but the Princess and Hamida never saw the beauty of the vale, the mountains, the lakes with their lotuses, the strange wooden houses with their rooftops covered with tulips and irises, the huge chenar or plane trees, the floating islands made of wood that had willows and vegetables growing on them, the hillsides covered with irises, the streams abounding in trout; on their way they learned that the Em- 145 peror had already gone from Kashmir to Kabul where they joined him so that the Princess had the consolation of seeing her home town again; it must, though, have been a ghost visit because who could have been left there for her now? Only memories of those graves in the Garden of Fidelity: Babur, Khanzada, Hindal; Dildar must have been dead too. A few old people might have been left who could have been talked to and Gulbadan could have walked on the ramparts of the Citadel; perhaps she took delight in memories when she saw a kite flown, a pigeon tumbling, heard the familiar dialect, but she was old now and Afghan winds are chill. She was probably glad when, in Hamida's train, she followed the Emperor back to Agra.

She had another grief to come, not only grief but shame, again, family shame. In 1594 the assayers of the royal mint were summoned, among them her own grandson, her daughter's son, Muhammad Yar. Funds were found to have been embezzled and 'by ill-fatedness' he and his companions fled to the hills. They were chased and caught; among their loot were fourteen rubies, a chapelet of choice pearls, embroidered jewels, robes, and much property. Most of the culprits were executed, but history does not say what happened to Muhammad Yar. Perhaps his grandmother saved him, but it can be guessed Gulbadan would have rather he were killed than left alive, disgraced.

She had, too, one more Khanzada-like task to do: as an old lady she, with Hamida, interceded with the Emperor for Prince Salim.

As his sons grew up, Akbar had become grievously disappointed in them. It was the old old story of drink and drugs, always Mughal indulgences—strange for strict followers of Muhammad. Over and over again Babur had renounced wine, that 'death in life;' his 'I renounced wine and ordered all my gold and silver goblets to be broken...the fragments to be given to the dervishes'—holy men—'and the poor,' had become almost familiar words. He had vowed he would give it up when he was forty and so, in his thirty-ninth year, drank

A chenar tree with squirrels

'copiously,' and still did not give it up; he even mixed drinking wine with drinking arrack, that most fiery and raw of spirits, and had to confess that it 'undid him,' but the vow he made before the battle of Khanua was different: this time the goblets and cups were really broken up; some of the wine was poured into the ground, the rest had salt thrown into it to make vinegar and Babur kept his promise—which was why Gulbadan saw the tank filled with lemonade—but he still took what he called ma'jun, which is hemp or hashish, called in India 'bhang' and violently intoxicating. Humayun could not exist without his opium.

Akbar alone was the exception—perhaps that Ganges water saved him—but of his three princely sons, Daniyal, the favourite, was to die of drink just before Akbar himself and had been for years so sodden with it that he was useless; Prince Murad, who had shown promise of inheriting his great-grandfather's genius as a military leader, died in terrible delirium tremens when he was only twenty-nine, but Salim, the eldest, was not only a drunkard—later, as the Emperor Jahangir, he was to boast that he drank forty-nine cups of wine a day—he also bedevilled his father in every way possible, offending, rebelling, even once trying to usurp the throne. He was also unattractive, sulky, moody, without restraint; at last Akbar banished him to Allahabad and it seemed likely that the throne would go to a grandson, perhaps to Salim's eldest son, Khusrau, of whom Salim was always jealous, or a younger son, Khurram, whom Akbar loved; yet, by tradition, Salim, as eldest son, was the rightful heir and the ladies did not believe he was as bad as was reputed. They knew Akbar was overweening and perhaps drove the young man to desperation—and so Hamida and Gulbadan brought their own special and distinguished pressure on Akbar to forgive this difficult son.

Hamida, Humayun's reluctant child-bride of sixty years ago, was now the energetic and powerful hub of the royal family life, far richer than Gulbadan, though the Princess too was given continual gifts of money and jewels; Hamida

Babur riding drunk through camp

gave magnificent feasts at her house for every family occasion —the marriages of the princes, the many births of the Emperor's grandchildren—and she was the right person to stage-manage the reconciliation between her son and grandson, the present and future emperors.

One of the 'royals' among the court ladies was sent to fetch Salim from Allahabad; the Prince was afraid to come but he was coaxed and soon, 'Hamida took his hand and cast him at the feet of the Emperor,' who could not resist this family occasion. He raised the Prince up 'lovingly;' perhaps the fact that Salim had confessed his evil deeds and had brought gifts, money and three hundred and fifty elephants, helped to mollify Akbar, and the generous Shahinshah, in order to capture the heart of the terrified Prince, took his own turban off his head and placed it on Salim's, which not only meant forgiveness but acknowledged the Prince as heir. Once again the ladies had triumphed, and altered the course of history.

* * *

Gulbadan's last years were not all worry and grief; there was still her love of Hamida and still many steadfast friends; there were still the feasts she loved and other court excitements. Probably one of the last she saw of these was a momentous elephant fight between those two inveterate rivals, Salim and his son Khusrau.

These fights, of which Akbar was so fond, often took place in an open space below the great red wall of the Fort at Agra from which the Emperor and Court could look down.

Elephants are usually peaceable animals, and sagacious. Akbar, for instance, had a 'punishment elephant' at Fathpur Sikri which was so wise that if the victim it was supposed to trample, though found guilty by the judge, was in reality innocent, the elephant would refuse to move and gently pushed the terrified man or woman aside with its trunk; but war, or fighting, elephants, were different, with long tusks, their feet heavily armour-toed and they were trained to battle;

besides this, before a fight, they were additionally maddened by the giving to them of bhang. They were prodded with spears as well as with the ankus, the short, sharp-headed goad with which the driver could prick their heads; they were also excited with fireworks. A fight was extremely dangerous; if the mahout were knocked off, or an attendant got in the way, there would be instant death as the opposing elephant would trample and beat with its trunk.

Abu'l Fazl tells the story of this fight in his Ain-i-Akbari, finished just a few years before his own violent death in 1602; mercifully Akbar never knew that this murder was the work of Salim. Always jealous, Salim was almost insanely so of Abu'l Fazl and believed, quite rightly, that he was advising the Emperor to pass over Salim's rights and name a different heir. Salim prevailed on the Raja of Orchha to waylay the courtier on his way back from the Deccan and kill him. Though Abu'l Fazl could have escaped from the ambush, he chose to stay and fight and was outnumbered. The Raja, who was plentifully rewarded, brought the head to Salim who gave it the final insult of throwing it into his privy.

'Salim had an elephant called Giranbar who was a match for any in Akbar's stable.' So runs Abu'l Fazl's account.

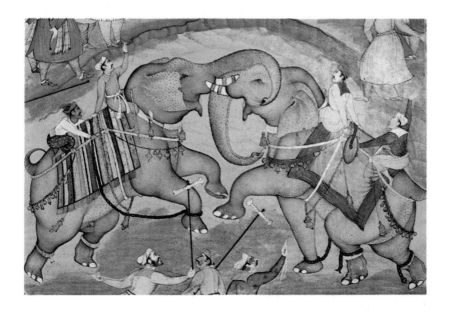

Khusrau announced that he also had one Abrup, which was as strong, or stronger, than Giranbar. To end the argument Akbar arranged for the pair to fight and watched the outcome from a balcony on the wall with Khusrau's younger brother Khurram beside him; it is sure that the ladies watched too from behind their screens. Salim and Khusrau were on horseback in the arena and, according to custom, a third elephant was there whose duty was to come to the help of either of the contestants if it was being too badly mauled.

Giranbar completely worsted Abrup and, as he mauled him terribly, the third elephant moved in, but Salim's men broke all the rules and pelted it with stones, wounding it and its driver badly; at once there was a foray between the princes and their supporters, disgraceful in an open tourney and in front of the crowd. Akbar immediately sent Khurram down to stop it; though only a boy and the fighters were his own father and his elder brother, Khurram managed to calm them; he tried to separate the elephants with fireworks, but they were too maddened; both Giranbar and Abrup ran away and threw themselves into the Jumna, which made Akbar even more angry. Finally Khusrau came up to the balcony and had the impudence to abuse Salim to the Emperor with unheard of rudeness. Akbar had to withdraw ill; in fact this brought on the first fierce attack of the dysentery that was eventually to kill him.

Though the ladies were distressed beyond measure, they were both deeply impressed by Khurram's dignity and grace and his authority, and as she watched the boy with pride, Gulbadan might have glimpsed the continuity of the dynasty she had loved and served so long: founded by Babur, almost lost by Humayun, made firm by Akbar, she knew now it would pass to Salim Jahangir and perhaps a hope stirred in her that by some miracle this boy, Khurram, in whom she saw such quality, would also succeed; in fact he did, by the early death of Khusrau, becoming the fifth Mughal Emperor, Shah Jahan.

She was not, of course, to see this. In February 1603, the same year that saw the death of Elizabeth the First of England, Gulbadan, at eighty, was smitten with a fatal fever. Hamida was with her in those last hours, as were a few of her old friends among the court ladies.

She lay with closed eyes but when Hamida whispered to her, using the affectionate 'Elder Sister,' Gulbadan opened her eyes and said, 'J'iu,' which is a small blessing or thanks from an older person to a younger one. Then she said, 'I die. You live.' It was her last quiet injunction.

There seems to have been no 'death name' for Gulbadan. Hamida was to be known as Miriam Makhani in tribute, oddly enough, to the Virgin Mary, but Gulbadan lives on in history as herself, Princess Rosebody.

Akbar himself helped to carry her bier.

List of Illustrations and Acknowledgements

(Or. 12988, f. 73a). Nizam, the water-carrier, helping Humayun to cross the Ganges in 1539.

p.85 Miniature (detail) from the British Library *Akbar-nama*, 1603-4 (Or. 12988, f. 125b).

p.87 Miniature (detail) from the British Library *Akbar-nama*, 1603-4 (Or. 12988, f. 59b). Humayun defeating Sultan Bahadur at Gujarat in 1535.

p.89 Miniature from the Victoria & Albert Museum dispersed *Babur-nama*, c. 1589 (I.M. 276-1913). Babur, with his architect, plans the Bagh-i Wafa near Jalalabad.

p.91 Miniature from the British Library *Akbar-nama*, 1603-4 (Or. 12988, f. 20b).

p.97 Miniature from the British Library *Akbar-nama*, 1603-4 (Or. 12988, f. 106a). Mirza Askari with his sword slung round his neck surrendering to Humayun at Kandahar in 1545.

p.103 Miniature from a *Baharistan* of Jami, 1595 (Bodleian Library, Oxford; Elliot 254, f. 42r). The story of the unfaithful wife.

p.105 Miniature (detail) from the Freer Gallery *Babur-nama*, c. 1590-5 (54.29).

p.108 Miniature from a *Baharistan* of Jami, 1595 (Bodleian Library, Oxford; Elliot 254, f. 9r). A mulla rebuking a dervish

p.111 Miniature from the British Library *Akbar-nama*, 1603-4 (Or. 12988, f. 158a). Bairam Khan watching Akbar learning to shoot.

p.113 Miniature (detail) from the Chester Beatty Library *Akbar-nama*, c. 1605 (MS.3, f. 18). The capture of Hemu at the battle of Panipat in 1556.

p.115 Miniature (detail) from the Victoria & Albert Museum *Akbar-nama*, c. 1590 (I.S. 2-1896, 9/117). The marriage of Baqi Muhammad Khan, eldest son of Maham Anaga, in 1561.

p.117 Miniature (detail) from the Victoria & Albert Museum *Akbar-nama*, c. 1590 (I.S. 2-1896 37/117). The beheading of a treacherous servant in the house of Khwaja M'uazzam in 1564, observed by woman from behind the screen.

p.119 Miniature from the Victoria & Albert Museum *Akbar-nama*, c. 1590 (I.S. 2-1896, 69/117). The immolation of the Rajput women during the siege of Chitor in 1567.

BIBLIOGRAPHY

Gulbadan Begam, *The History of Humayun* or *Humayun-nama*, tr. by A.S. Beveridge, Royal Asiatic Society, London 1902.

Babur, *Memoirs*, 2 vols., tr. by J. Leyden & W. Erskine, 1826, revised edition, Oxford 1921.

Jauhar, *Memoirs*, tr. by C. Stewart, London, 1832.

Lamb, Harold, *Babur the Tiger*, 1962.

Poole, S. Lane, *Babar* (*Rulers of India* series), London, 1899.

Abu'l Fazl, *The Akbar Nama*, 3 vols., tr. by H. Beveridge, Asiatic Society of Bengal, Calcutta, 1907-39.

Abu'l Fazl, *Ain-i-Akbari*, Vol.I, tr. by H. Blochmann, Calcutta, 1873.

Malleson, G.B., *Akbar* (*Rulers of India* series), London, 1890.

Prasad, Beni, *History of Jahangir*, Allahabad, 1930.

Pelsaert, F., *Jahangir's India* (*The Remonstratie of F.P.*), tr. from the Dutch by W.H. Moreland & P. Geyl, Cambridge, 1925.

Jahangir, *Tuzuk-i-Jahangiri*, 2 vols., tr. by A. Rogers & ed. by H. Beveridge, London 1909-14.

Ansari, M.A., *Social Life of the Mughal Emperors*, Allahabad, 1974.

Powell-Price, J.C., *A History of India*, London, 1955.

Gascoigne, B., *The Great Moghuls*, London, 1971.

Lewis, B. (editor), *The World of Islam*, London, 1976.

Manucci, N., *Storia do Mogor*, tr. by W. Irvine, London 1907.

Arberry, A.J., *The Golden Pomegranate*, a selection from the poetry of the Mogul Empire in India, London, 1966.

Guillaume, Alfred, *Islam*, London, 1956.

In this book, intended for the general reader, the publishers have followed the accepted practice of omitting diacritical marks from the transliterations of Oriental words. Those who wish to ascertain the full transliterations are directed to the primary sources listed in the Bibliography.

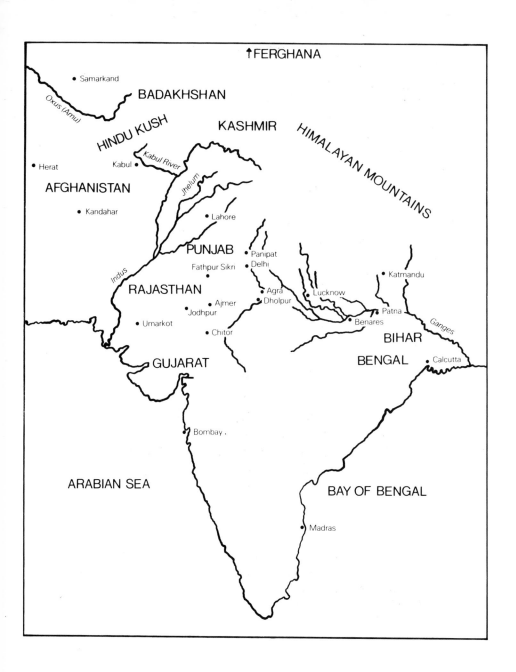

The publishers would like to thank the following for their kind permission to reproduce material in their collections: the curators of the Bodleian Library; the British Library; the Trustees of the British Museum; the Trustees of the Chester Beatty Library and Gallery of Oriental Art, Dublin; the Syndics of the Fitzwilliam Museum, Cambridge; the Smithsonian Institution, Freer Gallery of Art, Washington D.C.; the India Office Library and Records; the Keir Collection; Her Majesty Queen Elizabeth II for Her Gracious Permission to reproduce items in the Royal Library, Windsor (Copyright reserved); the School of African and Oriental Studies; Sotheby Parke Bernet & Co.; the Victoria & Albert Museum; the Walters Art Gallery, Baltimore.